# Street by Street

# SLOUGH, R
# MAIDENHEAD
## EGHAM, ETON, STAINES
Bray, Burnham, Cookham, Datchet, Englefield Green,
Holyport, Iver, Iver Heath, Langley, Old Windsor, Poyle

G000088823

**2nd edition January 2006**
© Automobile Association Developments Limited
2005

Original edition printed August 2002

**Ordnance Survey®** This product includes map data licensed from Ordnance Survey® with the permission of the Controller of Her Majesty's Stationery Office. © Crown copyright 2005. All rights reserved. Licence number 399221.

Published by AA Publishing (a trading name of Automobile Association Developments Limited, whose registered office is Fanum House, Basing View, Basingstoke, Hampshire RG21 4EA. Registered number 1878835).

Mapping produced by the Cartography Department of The Automobile Association. (A02546)

A CIP Catalogue record for this book is available from the British Library.

Printed by Oriental Press, Dubai

The contents of this atlas are believed to be correct at the time of the latest revision. However, the publishers cannot be held responsible or liable for any loss or damage occasioned to any person acting or refraining from action as a result of any use or reliance on any material in this atlas, nor for any errors, omissions or changes in such material. This does not affect your statutory rights. The publishers would welcome information to correct any errors or omissions and to keep this atlas up to date. Please write to Publishing, The Automobile Association, Fanum House (FH12), Basing View, Basingstoke, Hampshire, RG21 4EA.

Ref: ML180z

| | |
|---|---|
| Key to map pages | ii–iii |
| Key to map symbols | iv-1 |
| Enlarged map pages | 2-7 |
| Main map pages | 8-53 |
| Index – towns & villages | 54 |
| Index – streets | 54-60 |
| Index – featured places | 60-61 |
| Acknowledgements | 61 |

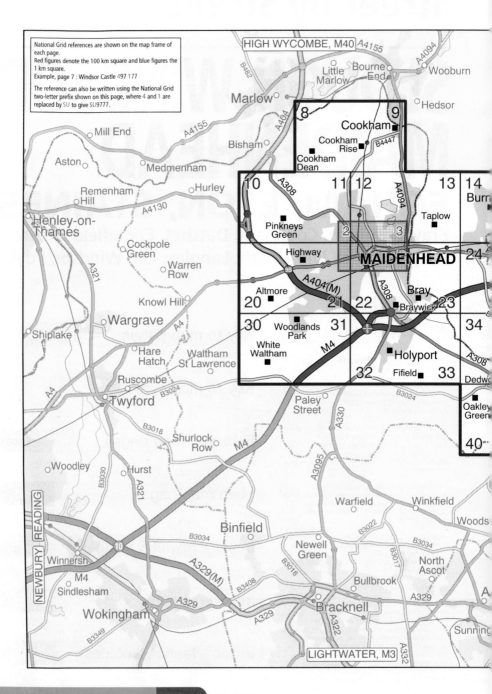

National Grid references are shown on the map frame of each page.
Red figures denote the 100 km square and blue figures the 1 km square.
Example, page 7 : Windsor Castle 497 177

The reference can also be written using the National Grid two-letter prefix shown on this page, where 4 and 1 are replaced by SU to give SU9777.

HIGH WYCOMBE, M40

**Enlarged scale pages**  **1:10,000**  6.3 inches to 1 mile

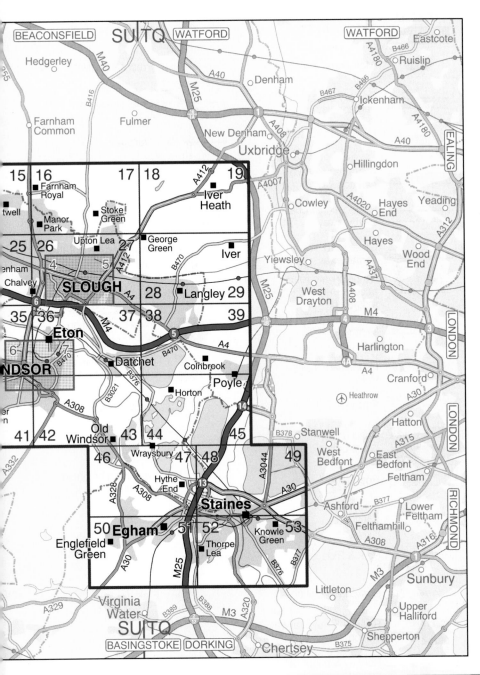

**iv**

| | | | |
|---|---|---|---|
| Junction 9 | Motorway & junction | ⊖ Light railway & station |
| Services | Motorway service area | +++++++++ Preserved private railway |
| | Primary road single/dual carriageway | LC Level crossing |
| Services | Primary road service area | •—•—•—• Tramway |
| | A road single/dual carriageway | ---------- Ferry route |
| | B road single/dual carriageway | ................ Airport runway |
| | Other road single/dual carriageway | — • — • • — County, administrative boundary |
| | Minor/private road, access may be restricted | ᵛᵛᵛᵛᵛᵛᵛᵛᵛᵛ Mounds |
| ← ← | One-way street | **17** Page continuation 1:15,000 |
| | Pedestrian area | **3** Page continuation to enlarged scale 1:10,000 |
| ----------- | Track or footpath | River/canal, lake, pier |
| ■■■■■■■ ■■■■■■■ | Road under construction | Aqueduct, lock, weir |
| ⌐ – – = = ⌐ | Road tunnel | 465 ▲ Winter Hill — Peak (with height in metres) |
| P | Parking | Beach |
| P+ | Park & Ride | Woodland |
| | Bus/coach station | Park |
| | Railway & main railway station | Cemetery |
| | Railway & minor railway station | Built-up area |
| ⊖ | Underground station | Featured building |

| | | | |
|---|---|---|---|
| ⊓⊓⊓⊓⊓⊓ | City wall | ♜ | Castle |
| A&E | Hospital with 24-hour A&E department | 🏛 | Historic house or building |
| PO | Post Office | Wakehurst Place NT | National Trust property |
| 📖 | Public library | Ⓜ | Museum or art gallery |
| 𝑖 | Tourist Information Centre | 🦅 | Roman antiquity |
| 𝑖 | Seasonal Tourist Information Centre | ⚱ | Ancient site, battlefield or monument |
| ⛽ ⛽ | Petrol station, 24 hour<br>Major suppliers only | 🏭 | Industrial interest |
| ✝ | Church/chapel | ❋ | Garden |
| 🚻 | Public toilets | ◉ | Garden Centre<br>Garden Centre Association Member |
| ♿ | Toilet with disabled facilities | 🌷 | Garden Centre<br>Wyevale Garden Centre |
| PH | Public house<br>AA recommended | 🌲 | Arboretum |
| 🍴 | Restaurant<br>AA inspected | 🛒 | Farm or animal centre |
| Madeira Hotel | Hotel<br>AA inspected | 🦌 | Zoological or wildlife collection |
| 🎭 | Theatre or performing arts centre | 🦜 | Bird collection |
| 🎥 | Cinema | 🦆 | Nature reserve |
| ⚑ | Golf course | 🐟 | Aquarium |
| ▲ | Camping<br>AA inspected | 🅥 | Visitor or heritage centre |
| 🚐 | Caravan site<br>AA inspected | ♈ | Country park |
| ▲🚐 | Camping & caravan site<br>AA inspected | ◠ | Cave |
| 🌴 | Theme park | 🌾 | Windmill |
| ⛪ | Abbey, cathedral or priory | 🛢 | Distillery, brewery or vineyard |

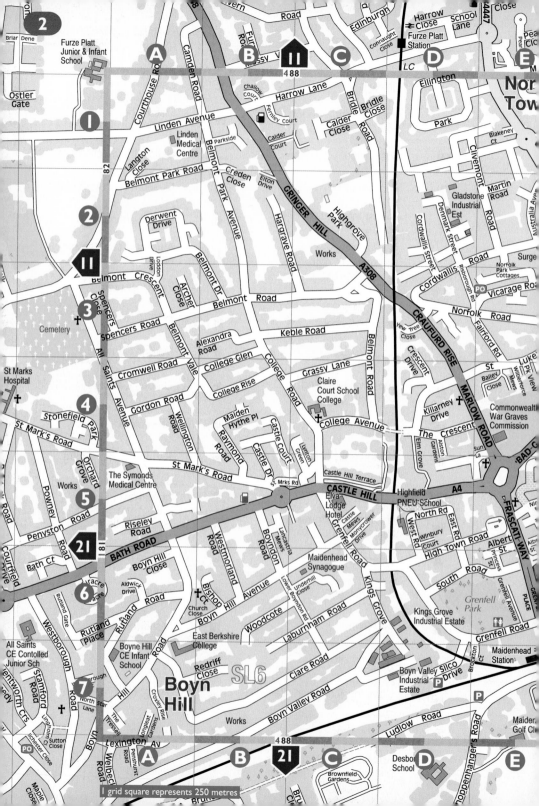

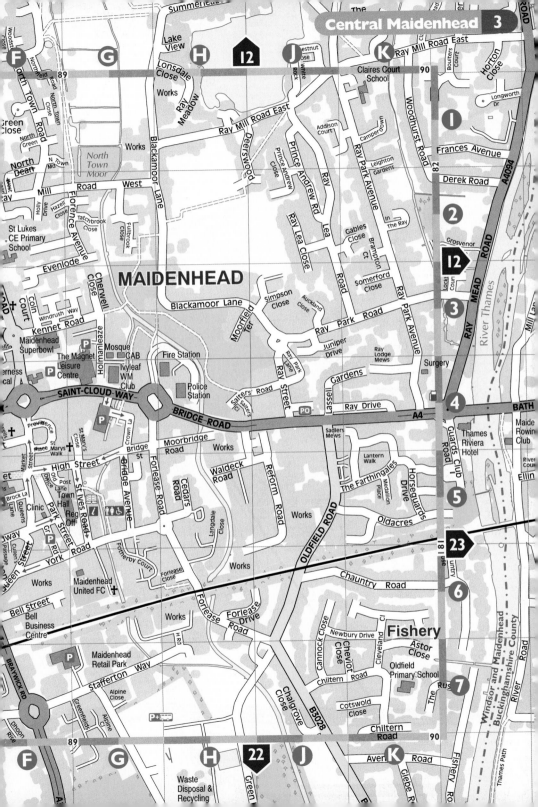

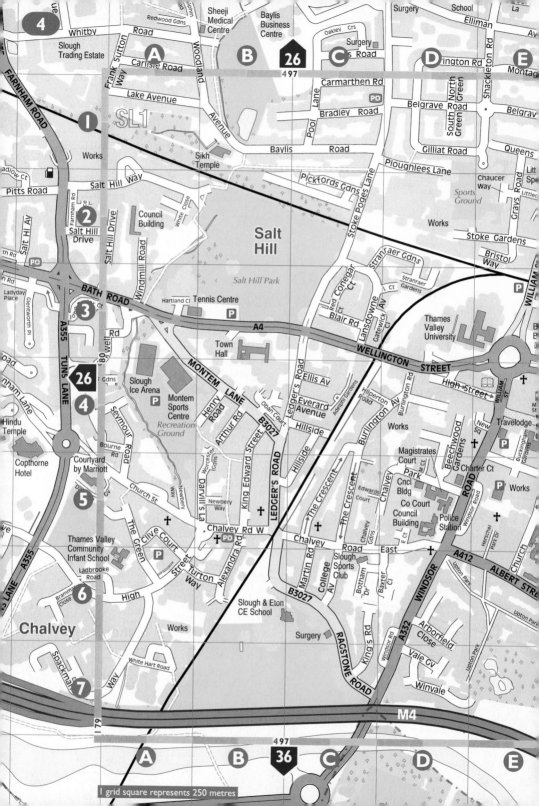

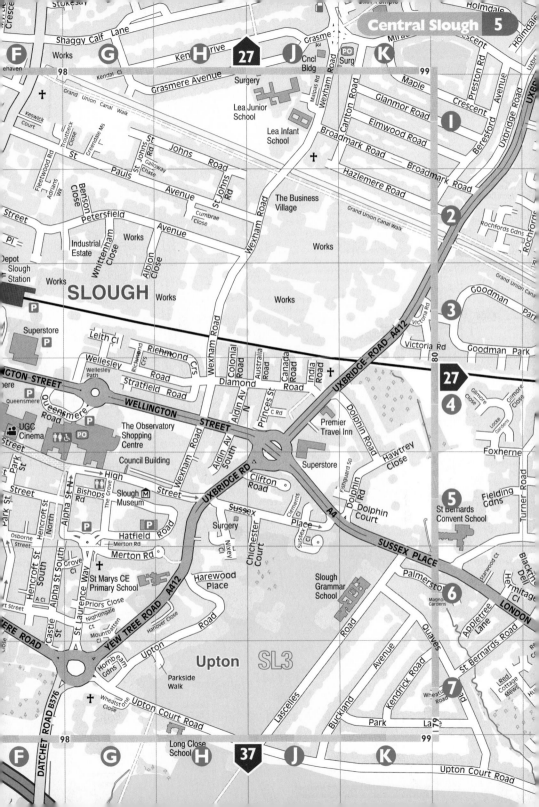

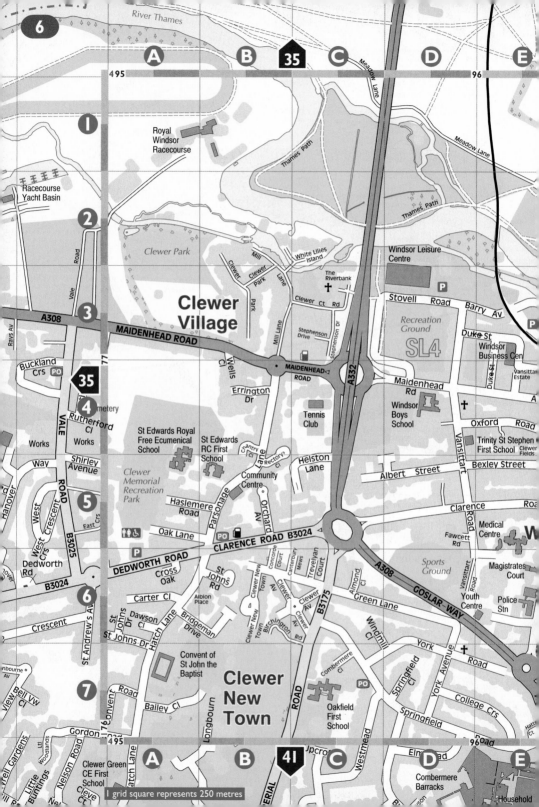

**6**

River Thames

A  B  **35**  C  D  E

495  96

**I**

Royal
Windsor
Racecourse

Racecourse
Yacht Basin

Thames Path

**2**

Clewer Park

White Lilies
Island

Windsor Leisure
Centre

The Riverbank

Meadow Lane

Thames Path

**Clewer
Village**

Clewer
Park
Lane

Clewer
Park

Mill
Lane

Clewer Ct Rd

P

Stovell   Road   Barry  Av

Recreation
Ground
**SL4**

Duke St

Windsor
Business Cen

Duke St

Vansittar
Estate

**3**  A308  **MAIDENHEAD ROAD**

Rays Av

Vale   Road

77

Wells   Cl

Stephenson
Drive

Stephenson Dr

MAIDENHEAD◁
ROAD

A332

Maidenhead
Rd

A

**35**  Buckland
Crs  PO

Errington
Dr

Tennis
Club

Windsor
Boys
School

Oxford   Road

Trinity St Stephen
First School  Clewer
Fields

**4**  Cemetery
Rutherford
Cl

VALE   ROAD

Works

Works

St Edwards Royal
Free Ecumenical
School

St Edwards
RC First
School

Cantry
Cl
Cl
Rectory

Helston
Lane

Vansittart

Albert  Street

Bexley Street

Shirley
Avenue

East Crs

Clewer
Memorial
Recreation
Park

Community
Centre

Clarence
Road

Medical
Centre

W

**5**  West
Crescent

Hanover

West
Crs

B3025

West
Way

Haslemere
Road

Parsonage
AV

Orchard
AV

Fawcett
Rd

Clarence   Road

Oak Lane

PO

**CLARENCE ROAD** B3024

Sports
Ground

Magistrates
Court

Dedworth
Rd

B3024

P

**DEDWORTH ROAD**

Cross
Oak

St
John's Rd

Concorde
Court

Canterbury
Mews

Trevelyan
Court

Almond
Cl

A308  GOSLAR  WAY

Youth
Centre

Police
Stn

**6**  St Andrew's Av

Crescent

Carter Cl

St
Johns
Dr  Dawson
Cl

Hatch Lane

Albion
Place

Bridgeman
Drive

Clewer New
Town

Clewer
AV

Clewer New
Town

Birchington

Clewer
AV
Rd

B3175

Green  Lane

Windmill
Cl

York   Road

York  Avenue

Springfield
Cl

View
Cl

Bell Vw
Cl

St Johns Dr

Convent of
St John the
Baptist

Combermere
Cl

Combermere

PO

Springfield

College Crs

**7**

nbourne
Av

Little
Buntings

Convent   Road

Bailey Cl

Longbourn

**Clewer
New
Town**

Oakfield
First
School

York

Springfield
Road

Gordon   Road

Woodlands

Nelson Road

495  96  Road

A  B  **41**  C  D  E

Little
Field Gardens

Clewer Green
CE First
School

Hatch Lane

Cleve La

ERIAL

Upcro

Westmead

Elm

Combermere
Barracks

Household

**1 grid square represents 250 metres**

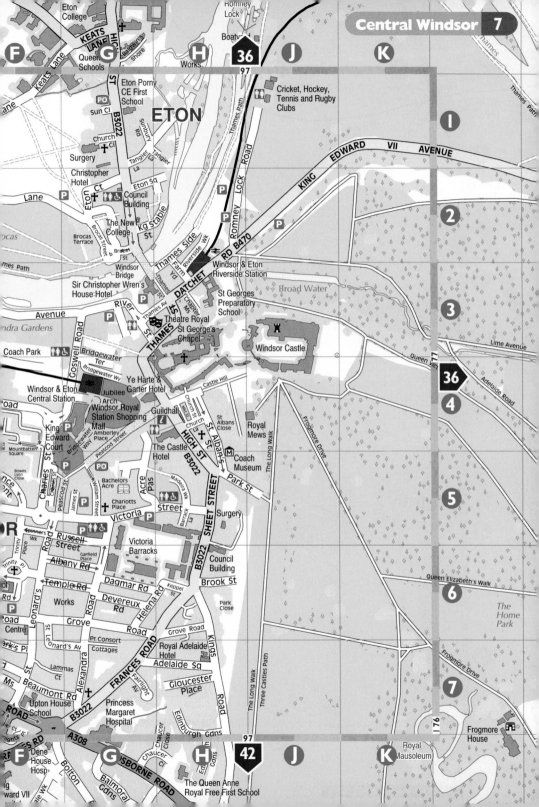

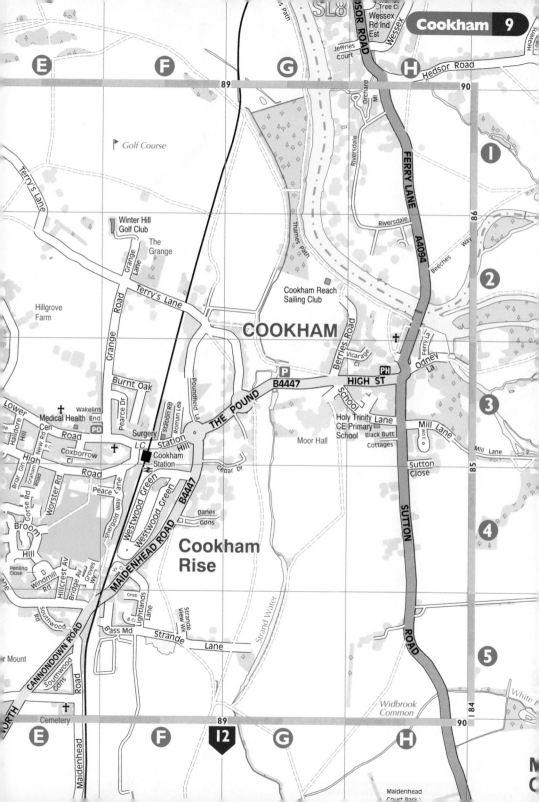

E  F  G  H

89  90

I

Golf Course

86

2

Terry's Lane

Winter Hill
Golf Club

The
Grange

Grange Road

Terry's Lane

Hillgrove
Farm

Thames Path

Cookham Reach
Sailing Club

**COOKHAM**

Riversdale

Riversdale

FERRY LANE

A4094

Beeches Way

Ferry La

Odney

Orchard Ml

3

Berries Road

Vicarage

SL8

Tree Cl

Wessex
Rd Ind
Est

Jeffries
Court

Hedsor Road

WINDSOR ROAD

Wessex

Heavens

Lower

Medical Health
Cen

Wakelins
End

PO

Coxborrow
Cl

High

Road

Worster Rd

Peace La

Burnt Oak

Pearce Dr

Station Rd

Roman Lea

LC

Station

Hill

Cookham
Station

Poundfield La

THE POUND

B4447

P

Moor Hall

Cedar Dr

School

HIGH ST

PH

Holy Trinity
CE Primary
School

Black Butt
Cottages

School Lane

Mill Lane

Mill Lane

Sutton
Close

85

3

4

Haldore

Hill

Briar Cln

Graham

Road

New Rd

R Cl

Corse Rd

Broom

Hill

Penling
Close

Windmill
Rd

Hillcrest Av

Bridge Av

Groves
Wy

Southwood
Rd

Southwood
Gdns

Road

CANNONDOWN ROAD

URTH

Cemetery

Maidenhead

MAIDENHEAD ROAD

Shergold Way Lane

Westwood Green

Westwood Green

B4447

Danes
Gdns

Gnsb

Lightlands
Lane

Strande
View Wk

Bass Md

Strande

Lane

**Cookham
Rise**

Strand Water

SUTTON

ROAD

Widbrook
Common

White

84

4

5

E  F  G  H

89  90

Maidenhead
Court Park

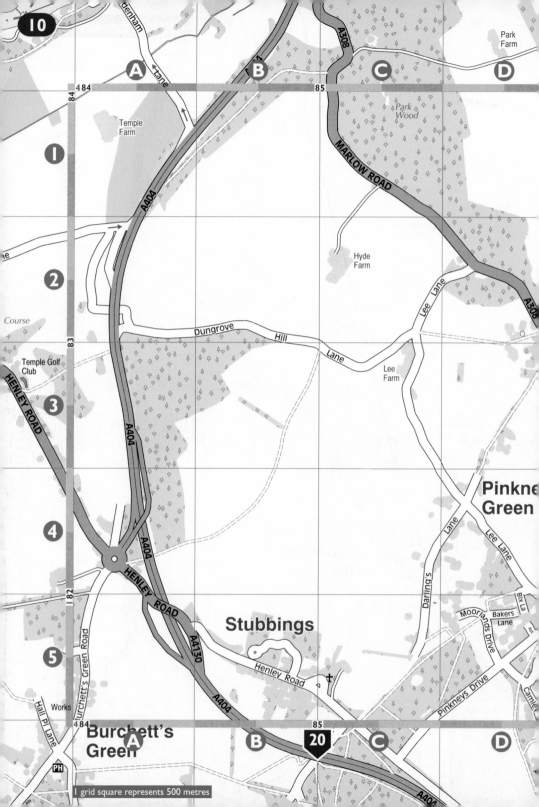

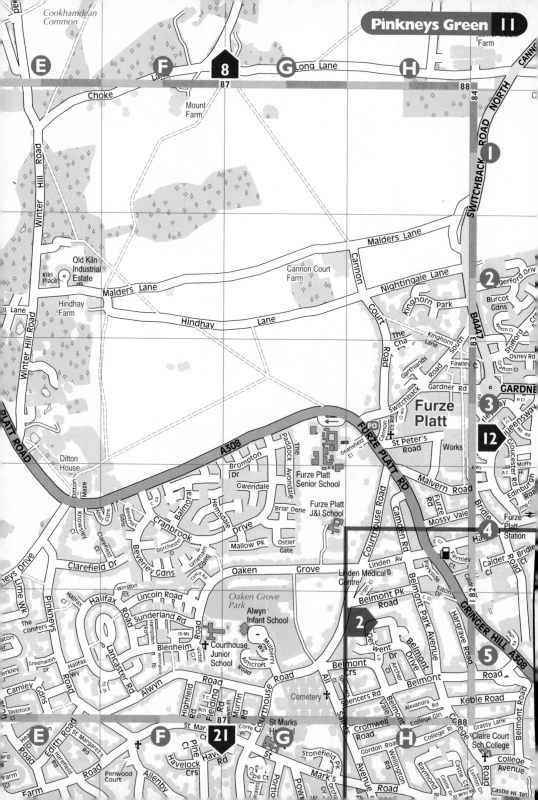

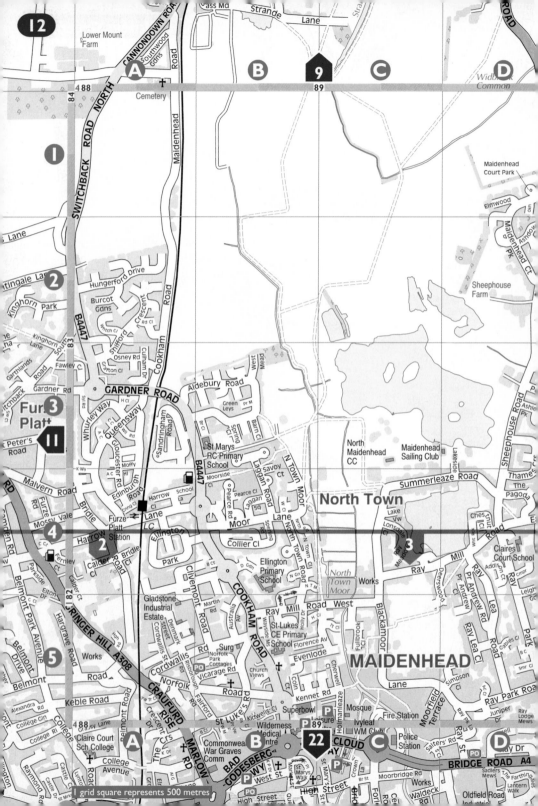

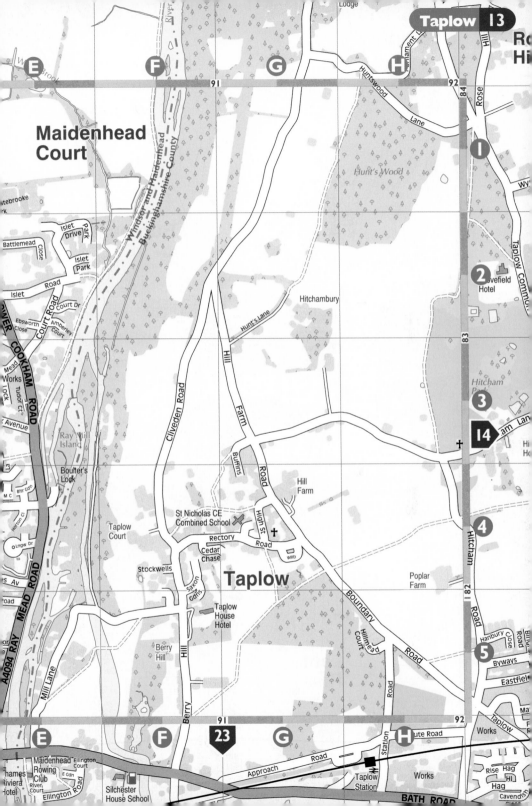

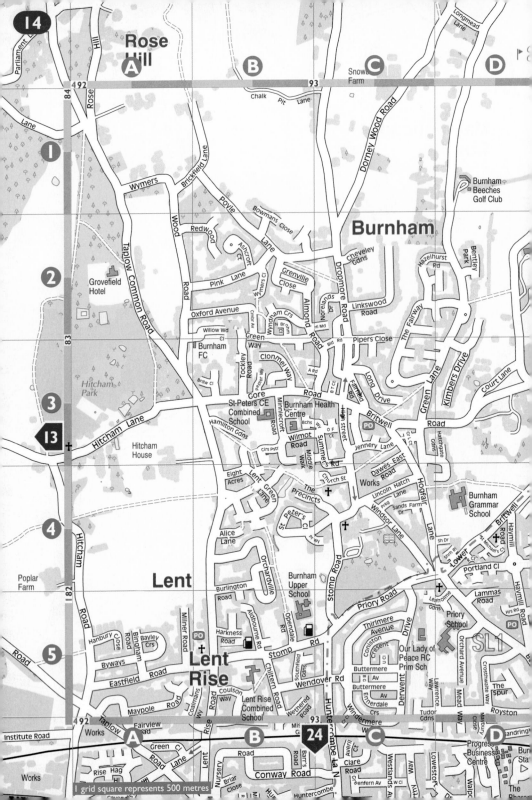

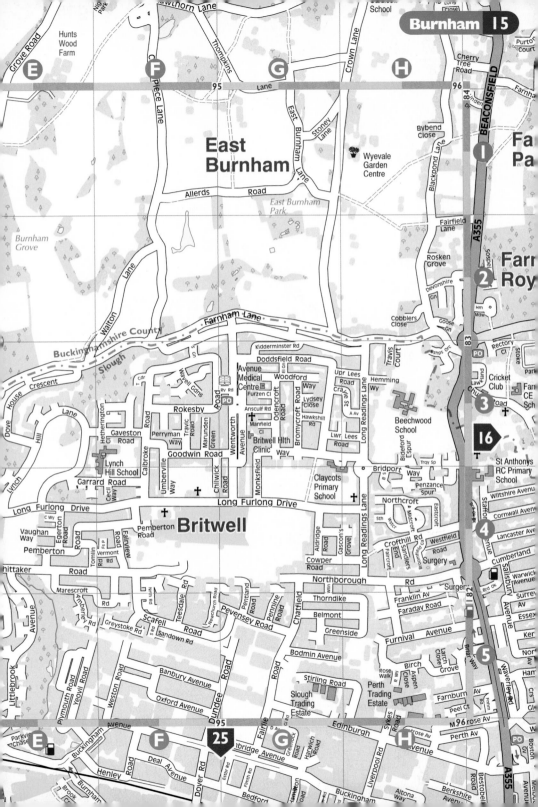

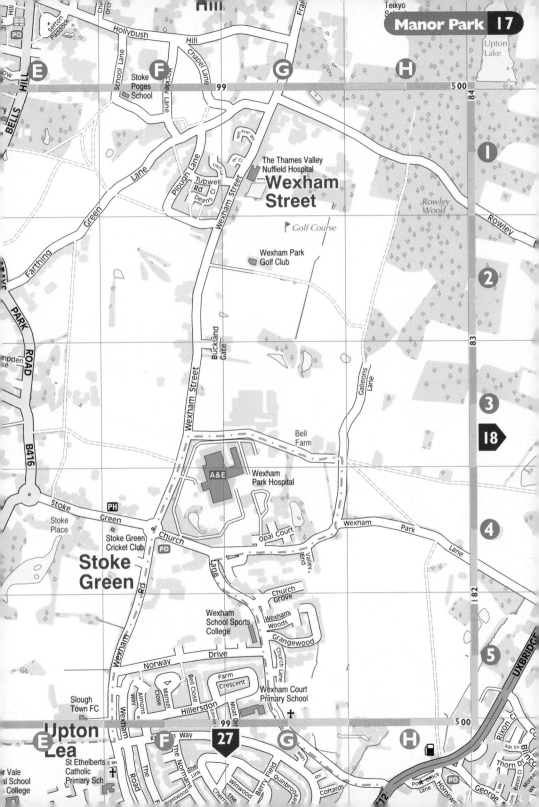

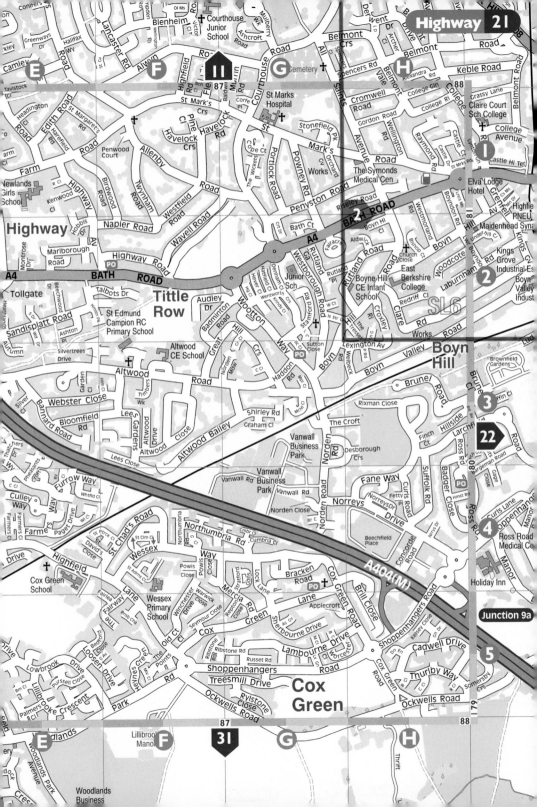

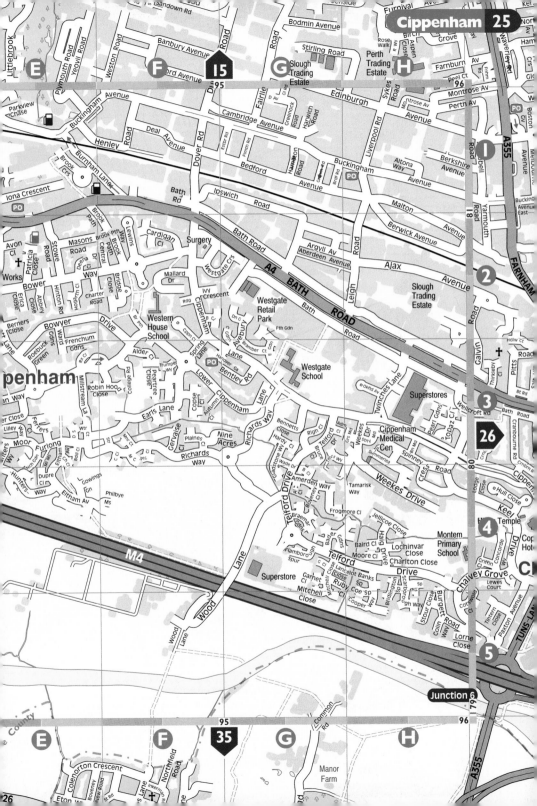

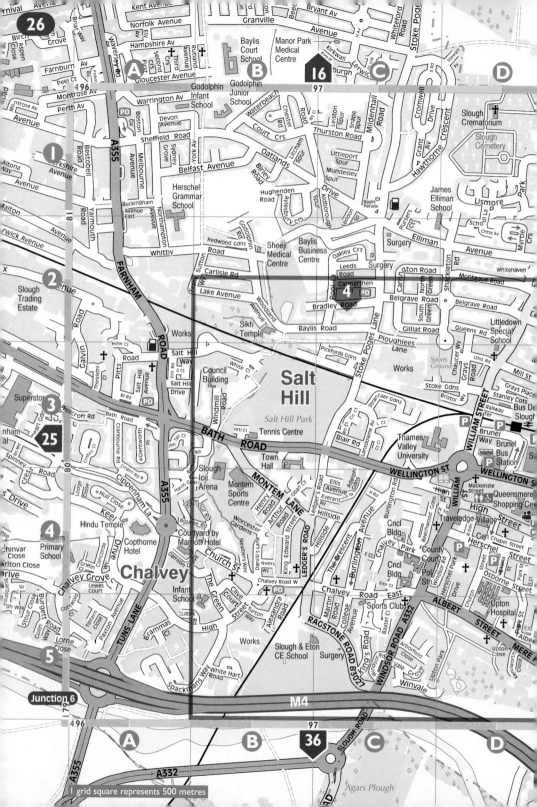

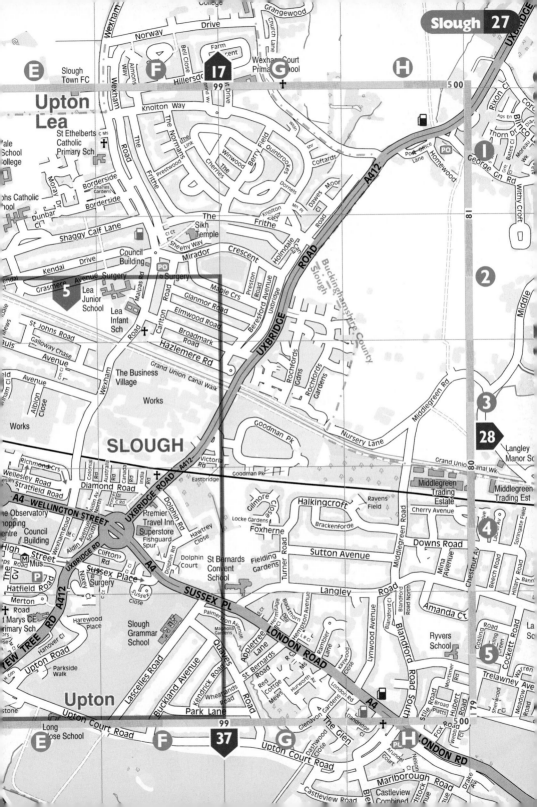

Coppins

Lane

Beeches Way

Heath
Lodge

Low Street

Green Lane

SLO

Coppi

Iver Ldg

Swan Road

**E**  **F**  **19**  **G**  **H**

Love
Green

Wood Lane

Love Lane

Barnfield Road

Evreham
Road

Cecil Rd

Iver

B 470

**I**

Iver Village
Junior School

Stonecroft Av

Widecroft Rd

PO

**B470**

**HIGH ST**

Surgery

Swan Road

ing

Honeysuckle
lose

Lane

**B470** **LANGLEY PARK ROAD**

Iverdale Cl

Leacroft Road

Leas

Drive

Reed Cl

Reed Cl

Dutton Way

Grange Way

Iver Village
Infant School

Blythe Cl

Ward
Close

Works

**B470**

Colne Orch

Holmsdale

Thorney

Road

Victoria
Crs

Marina Way

**2**

Barnes
Way

North
Lane

Mansion

Lane

Trading
Estate

Ridge

Way

Court

**3**

Grand Union Canal

Hollow Hl Lane

Grand Union Canal Walk

Works

Iver Station

Bathurst

Walk

PO

Bathurst
Close

Thorney Lane South

**80**

**4**

Thorne

St James
Walk

Syke Cluan

Syke Ings

Bathurst

Avenue

Somerset Way

Wellesley

Richings Park
Sports Club

Way

**5**

Richings
Park

North
Pk

Richings

St Leonards
Walk

Thorney House

Thorne

Lane

Parlaunt Road

Main Dr

**E**  **F**  **39**  **G**  **H**

Deverills
Wy

Stornaway Rd

Kmp C

The Poynings

The
Ridings

Slade

Old

Richings Park Golf

Old Cl
Lambourne Drive
Ribstone Rd
Ribstone Rd
Russet Rd
Shoppenhangers
Tressmill Drive
Road
**Cox Green**
Thurlby Way
Somersby
wells Road

Lowbrook
Haynes
Green
The Points
Rd
**21**
Rylstone
Close
Road

Woodlands
Woodlands Avenue
Crescent
Phipps Close
Palme
ke Crescent
Park

Lillibrooke Manor

**E**  **F**  **G**  **H**

**I**

Woodlands
Business
Park

Thrift Lane

eywood Avenue

oodlands
ark CP
chool

Snowball Hill

Heywood Farm

Thrift Lane

**2**

**M4**

**3**

**32**

Stu

**4**

Foxley Green Farm

Paley Street

**5**

A330

**Touchen-end**

**E**  **F**  **G**  **H**

Littlefield Green

B3024

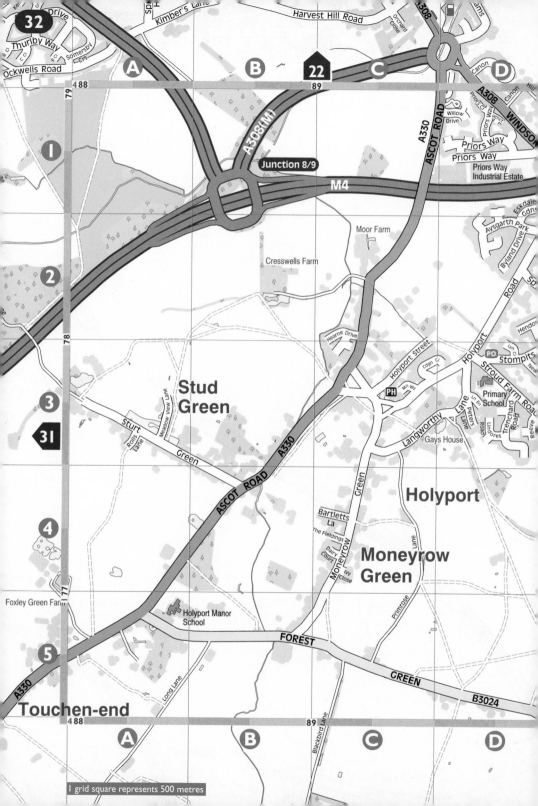

E F **25** G H Junction 6

95 96 79

**Eton Wick**

Colenorton Crescent
Boveney New Road
Northfield Road
Inkerman Rd
Moores Lane
Alma Road
Eton Wick Road
Vaughan Gardens
Bell
PO
Wenlock
The Walk
Albert Pl
Common
Sheepcote Rd

26

Tilstone Avenue
Leeson Gdns
Tilstone Close
Cornwall
Victoria Road
Princes Close
Queens Road
Hayward's Mead
Haywards Md
Eton Wick FC
ETON

Eton Wick CE First School

**WICK** Bunces Close

Manor Farm

Road

A355

Broken Furlong

Somervil
Stroud
Eisenhower
Place

**2**

78

**ROAD**

**South Field**

Thames Path

River Thames

Path

Boveney Lock

Royal Windsor Racecourse

Meadow Lane

A332

South M

E T

**3**

**36**

Marina

Racecourse Yacht Basin

Sutherland Grange

P

Willow Place

White Lillies Island
The Riverbank
Clewer Park Lane
Mill Lane
Clewer Rd
Stephenson Drive
Stovell Road

Windsor Leisure Centre

Barry Av

P

**4**

Barr

Rec Grnd

Duke St

Windsor Bus Cen

**IDENHEAD** **ROAD**

A308

**Clewer**
**Village** **6**

VALE RD

Whiteley
Aston Mead
Hylle Close
Cawcott Drive
Needham
Jacob
Burnetts Road
Thames Mead
North Close
Harcourt Road
Tudor Way
Losfield Road
Surly Hall Walk
Loring Rd
C Cl
St George's Close
Mansell
Stuart Way
Dedworth Drive
Hanover Way
West Crescent
B3025
East Crs

Sawyer's Close
Buckland Crescent
PO
Rutherford Close
Shirley Av
Community Centre
Cemetery
Works

Rays Avenue
Wells Close
Errington Dr

Parsonage Lane

Maidenhead Road

Windsor Boys School
Vansittart

Arthur
Ind
Est
Rd

Oxford Rd
Trinity St Stephen First School
Bexley Street

**5**

St Edwards Royal Free Ecumenical School
St Edwards RC First Sch
Clewer Memorial Rec Park
Haslemere Road
Oak Lane
PO

Tennis Club

Chantry
Rectory
Helston Lane
Orchard Avenue

Albert Street

Road

Clarence

Fawcett Rd

Medical Centre

Dedworth County Middle School
Smiths Lane
School

Stuart Way
Manor Road
Church Terrace
Greenacre
Greaves Lane
Cranbourne Avenue

**41**

DEDWORTH RD

Andrews Avenue
St Johns Drive
Cross Oak
Carter Close
Dawson Close
Bridgeman Drive

**CLARENCE**

Albion Place

Clewer New Town

Convent of St John the Baptist

Trevelyan Middle School

ROAD

Clewer Av

Green

Almond

Vansittart Road

Sports Grnd

Magistrates Court
Police Station
Youth Centre

GOSLAR WAY A308

Lane

York Road

Windmill

Cnbmhr
York
Ighfield

St M

95 96

I grid square represents 500 metres

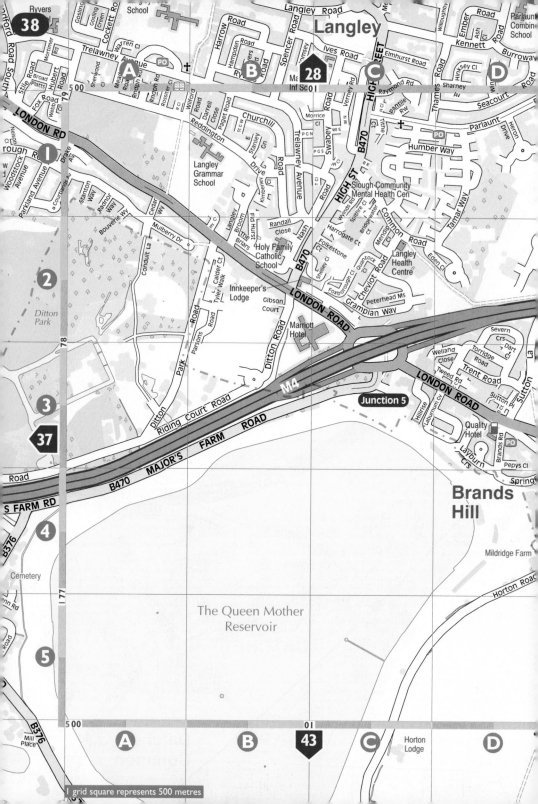

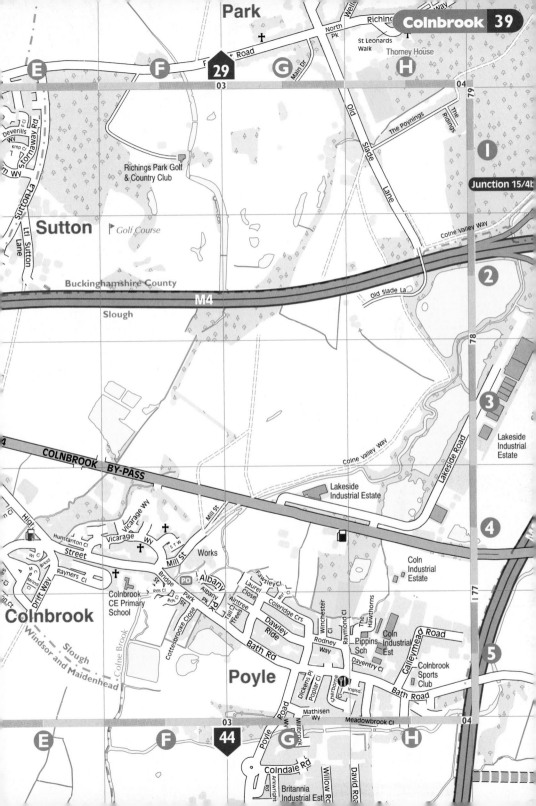

**Park**

Richings

Wells Way

North Pk

St Leonards Walk

Thorney House

E    F    **29**    G    H

03    04    79

Richings Park Golf & Country Club

The Poynlings

The Ridings

I

**Sutton**    ▶ *Golf Course*

Junction 15/4b

Stornaway Rd

Sutton La

Ltl Sutton Lane

Deverills Wy

kmp Cl

m Wy

Old Slade Lane

Colne Valley Way

Buckinghamshire County

Old Slade La

2

**M4**

Slough

78

COLNBROOK BY-PASS

Colne Valley Way

3

Lakeside Industrial Estate

Lakeside Industrial Estate

Lakeside Road

4

High Cl

n Cl

Vicarage Wy

Vicarage Wy

Vicarage

Mill St

Mill St

S T W

Works

Coln Industrial Estate

Hunstanton Cl

Street

Rayners Cl

Wl Cl

Brksdl

M Cl

Mrind

Drift Way

Bridge St

Rds Cl

**PO**

Park St

Albany

Albany Pk Rd

Fawsley Cl

Laurel Close

Aintree Cl

Coleridge Crs

Winchester Cl

Raymond Cl

The Hawthorns

Coln Industrial Est

Calleywead Road

**Colnbrook**

Colnbrook CE Primary School

Cottebrooke Close

Colne Brook

Windsor and Maidenhead

Slough

Dawley Ride

Bath Rd

Rodney Way

Pippins Sch

Daventry Cl

Coln Industrial Est

Colnbrook Sports Club

Bath Road

**Poyle**

Dickens Pl

Poplar Cl

Sherborne Cl

Inglsd.

Mathisen Wy

Meadowbrook Cl

E    F    **44**    G    H

03    04

Poyle Road

Millbrook Wy

Coldale Rd

Arkwright Rd

Willow Rd

David Rd

Britannia Industrial Est

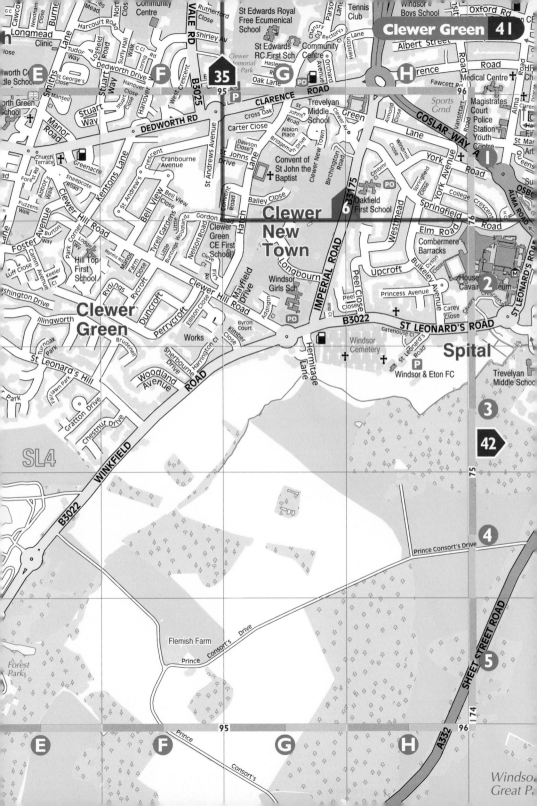

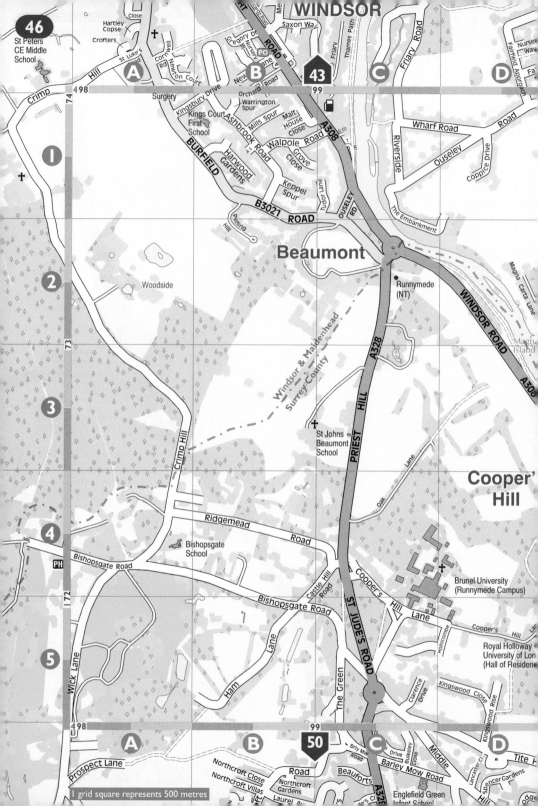

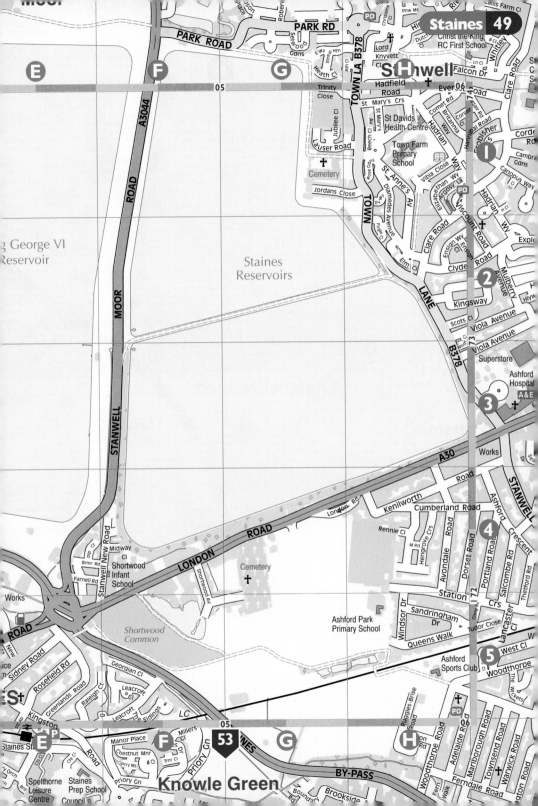

**Grid references (top):** E F G

Park Road / PARK RD

Christ the King RC First School

S**H**well

Town Farm Primary School

St Davids Health Centre

Cemetery

Jordans Close

King George VI Reservoir

Staines Reservoirs

**I**

**2**

Kingsway

Viola Avenue

Superstore

Ashford Hospital A&E

**3**

Works

Kenilworth

Cumberland Road

Rennie Cl

Station

**4**

STANWELL

Ashford Sports Club

West Cl

**5**

Woodthorpe

Stanwell New Road

Midway Cl

Shortwood Infant School

Shortwood Common

London Road

Cemetery

Ashford Park Primary School

Sandringham Dr

Queens Walk

Works

Sidney Road

Rosefield Rd

Greenlands Road

Leacroft

Kingston

**E P**

Staines St

Spelthorne Leisure Centre

Staines Prep School

Manor Place

Chestnut Mnr

Priory Gn

**F**

**53**

**G**

**H**

Knowle Green

BY-PASS

Woodthorpe Road

Adelaide Road

Marlborough Road

Townsend Road

Warwick Road

Ferndale Road

Brookside

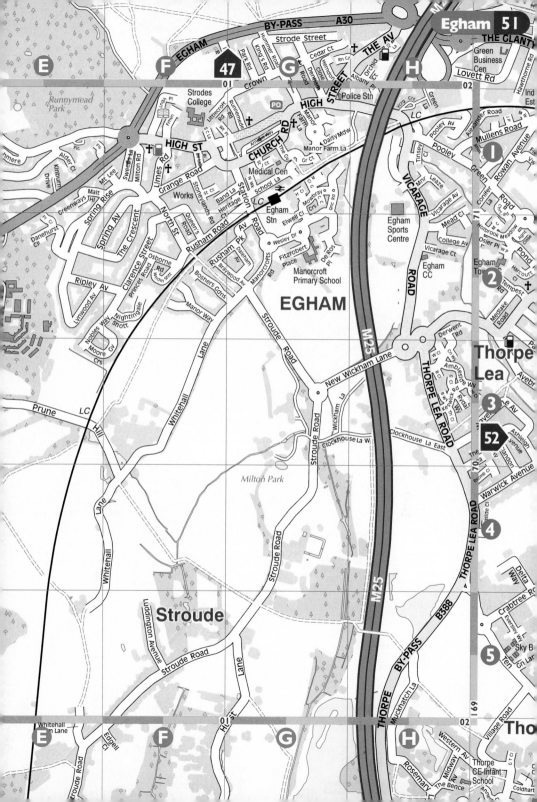

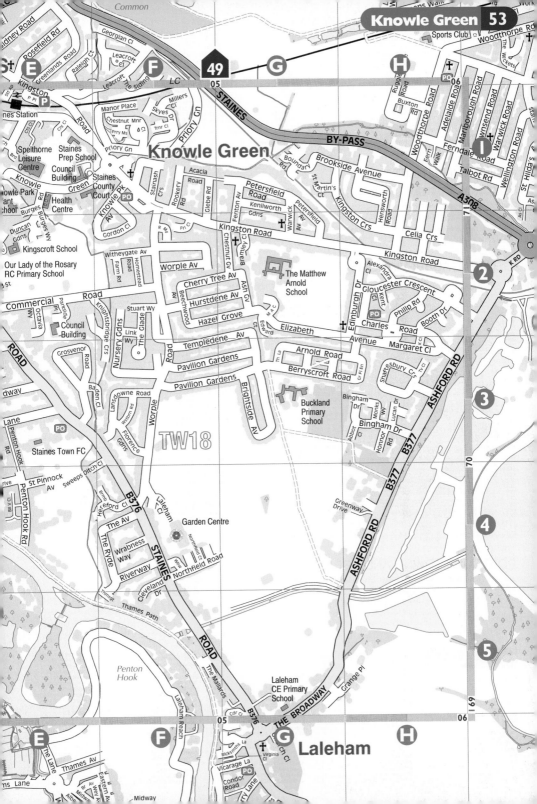

**Altmore** 20 C4
**Beaumont** 46 B2
**Bigfrith** 8 A4
**Boveney** 34 C3
**Boyn Hill** 2 A7
**Brands Hill** 38 D4
**Bray** 23 F5
**Bray Wick** 22 C4
**Britwell** 15 F4
**Burchett's Green** 20 A1
**Burnham** 14 C2
**Chalvey** 26 A4
**Cippenham** 24 D3
**Clewer Green** 41 E2
**Clewer New Town** 6 B7
**Clewer Village** 6 A3
**Colnbrook** 39 E5
**Cookham** 9 G2
**Cookham Dean** 8 B3
**Cookham Rise** 9 F4
**Cooper's Hill** 46 D4
**Cox Green** 21 G5
**Datchet** 37 F5
**Datchet Common** 43 G1
**Dedworth** 34 D5
**Dorney** 24 B5
**Dorney Reach** 23 H5
**East Burnham** 15 F1
**Egham** 51 G2
**Egham Hythe** 52 B2
**Englefield Green** 50 B3
**Eton** 7 G1
**Eton Wick** 35 F1
**Farnham Park** 16 A1
**Farnham Royal** 16 A2
**Fifield** 33 F5
**Fishery** 3 K6
**Furze Platt** 11 H3
**George Green** 18 A5
**Highway** 21 E2
**Holloway** 20 A3
**Holyport** 32 C4
**Horton** 44 C2
**Hythe End** 47 H4
**Iver** 29 H1
**Iver Heath** 19 F1
**Knowle Green** 53 F1
**Lake End** 24 B4
**Langley** 28 B5
**Lent** 14 A4
**Lent Rise** 14 A5
**Littlefield Green** 30 D5
**Littlewick Green** 20 A3
**Love Green** 19 F5
**Maidenhead** 3 G3
**Maidenhead Court** 13 E1
**Manor Park** 16 A4
**Middle Green** 28 A2
**Moneyrow Green** 32 C4
**North Town** 2 E1
**Oakley Green** 40 A1
**Old Windsor** 43 F5
**Pinkneys Green** 10 D4
**Poyle** 39 G5
**Richings Park** 29 G5
**Salt Hill** 4 B2
**Shreding Green** 28 D1
**Slough** 5 G3
**South Field** 35 H2
**Spital** 41 H3
**Staines** 48 D5
**Stoke Green** 17 E4
**Stroude**
**Stubbings**
**Stud Green**
**Sunnymeads**
**Sutton**
**Taplow**
**Thorpe Lea**
**Tittle Row**
**Touchen-end**
**Upton**
**Upton Lea**
**Wexham Street**
**White Waltham**
**Windsor**
**Woodlands Park**
**Woolley Green**
**Wraysbury**


# USING THE STREET INDEX

Street names are listed alphabetically. Each street name is followed by its postal town or area locality, the Postcode District, the page number, and the reference to the square in which the name is found.

Standard index entries are shown as follows:

**Abbey Cl** *SL* SL1 ..............................**25** E2

Street names and selected addresses not shown on the map due to scale restrictions are shown in the index with an asterisk:

**Alyson Ct** *MDHD* SL6 * ......................**3** F1

# GENERAL ABBREVIATIONS

ACC ACCESS
ALY ALLEY
AP APPROACH
AR ARCADE
ASS ASSOCIATION
AV AVENUE
BCH BEACH
BLDS BUILDINGS
BND BEND
BNK BANK
BR BRIDGE
BRK BROOK
BTM BOTTOM
BUS BUSINESS
BVD BOULEVARD
BY BYPASS
CATH CATHEDRAL
CEM CEMETERY
CEN CENTRE
CFT CROFT
CH CHURCH
CHA CHASE
CHYD CHURCHYARD
CIR CIRCLE
CIRC CIRCUS
CL CLOSE
CLFS CLIFFS
CMP CAMP
CNR CORNER
CO COUNTY
COLL COLLEGE
COM COMMON
COMM COMMISSION
CON CONVENT
COT COTTAGE
COTS COTTAGES
CP CAPE
CPS COPSE
CR CREEK
CREM CREMATORIUM
CRS CRESCENT
CSWY CAUSEWAY
CT COURT
CTRL CENTRAL
CTS COURTS
CTYD COURTYARD
CUTT CUTTINGS
CV COVE
CYN CANYON
DEPT DEPARTMENT
DL DALE
DM DAM
DR DRIVE
DRO DROVE
DRY DRIVEWAY
DWGS DWELLINGS
E EAST
EMB EMBANKMENT
EMBY EMBASSY
ESP ESPLANADE
EST ESTATE
EX EXCHANGE
EXPY EXPRESSWAY
EXT EXTENSION
F/O FLYOVER
FC FOOTBALL CLUB
FK FORK
FLD FIELD
FLDS FIELDS
FLS FALLS
FLS FLATS
FM FARM
FT FORT
FWY FREEWAY
FY FERRY
GA GATE
GAL GALLERY
GDN GARDEN
GDNS GARDENS
GLD GLADE
GLN GLEN
GN GREEN
GND GROUND
GRA GRANGE
GRG GARAGE
GT GREAT
GTWY GATEWAY
GV GROVE
HGR HIGHER
HL HILL
HLS HILLS
HO HOUSE
HOL HOLLOW
HOSP HOSPITAL
HRB HARBOUR
HTH HEATH
HTS HEIGHTS
HVN HAVEN
HWY HIGHWAY
IMP IMPERIAL
IN INLET
IND EST INDUSTRIAL ESTATE
INF INFIRMARY
INFO INFORMATION
INT INTERCHANGE
IS ISLAND
JCT JUNCTION
JTY JETTY
KG KING
KNL KNOLL
L LAKE
LA LANE
LDG LODGE
LGT LIGHT
LK LOCK
LKS LAKES
LNDG LANDING
LTL LITTLE
LWR LOWER
MAG MAGISTRATE
MAN MANSIONS
MD MEAD
MDW MEADOWS
MEM MEMORIAL
MKT MARKET
MKTS MARKETS
ML MALL
ML MILL
MNR MANOR
MS MEWS
MSN MISSION
MT MOUNT
MTN MOUNTAIN
MTS MOUNTAINS
MUS MUSEUM
MWY MOTORWAY
N NORTH
NE NORTH EAST
NW NORTH WEST
O/P OVERPASS
OFF OFFICE
ORCH ORCHARD
OV OVAL
PAL PALACE
PAS PASSAGE
PAV PAVILION
PDE PARADE
PH PUBLIC HOUSE
PK PARK
PKWY PARKWAY
PL PLACE
PLN PLAIN
PLNS PLAINS
PLZ PLAZA
POL POLICE STATION
PR PRINCE
PREC PRECINCT
PREP PREPARATORY
PRIM PRIMARY
PROM PROMENADE
PRS PRINCESS
PRT PORT
PT POINT
PTH PATH
PZ PIAZZA
QD QUADRANT
QU QUEEN
QY QUAY
R RIVER
RBT ROUNDABOUT
RD ROAD
RDG RIDGE
REP REPUBLIC
RES RESERVOIR
RFC RUGBY FOOTBALL CLUB
RI RISE
RP RAMP
RW ROW
S SOUTH
SCH SCHOOL
SE SOUTH
SER SERVICE
SH S
SHOP SHOP
SKWY SKY
SMT SU
SOC SO
SP
SPR SP
SQ SQU
ST ST
STN STA
STR STR
STRD STR
SW SOUTH
TDG TRA
TER TERR
THWY THROUGH
TNL TUN
TOLL TOLL
TPK TURN
TR TR
TRL T
TWR TO
U/P UNDER
UNI UNIVER
UPR UP
V
VA VA
VIAD VIAD
VIL V
VIS V
VLG VIL
VLS VI
VW V
W W
WD W
WHF WH
WK W
WKS W
WLS W
WY
YD Y
YHA YOUTH HOS

# POSTCODE TOWNS AND AREA ABBREVIATIONS

ASHF Ashford (Surrey)
BNEND Bourne End
CHERT Chertsey
DTCH/LGLY Datchet/Langley
EGH Egham
IVER Iver
MDHD Maidenhead
MLW Marlow
SL Slough
SLN Slough north
STA Staines
STWL/WRAY Stanwell/Wraysbury
VW Virginia W
WDSR Win

## Abb - Arg



## A


**Abbey Cl** *SL* SL1 25 E2
**Abbot Cl** *STA* TW18 53 H3
**Abbot's Wk** *WDSR* SL4 41 E1
**Abbotts Wy** *SL* SL1 24 D3
**Abell Gdns** *MDHD* SL6 11 E4
**Aberdeen Av** *SL* SL1 25 G2
**Acacia Av** *STWL/WRAY* TW19 44 A3
**Acacia Rd** *STA* TW18 53 F1
**Acre Pas** *WDSR* SL4 7 G5
**Adam Cl** *SL* SL1 25 G3
**Addington Cl** *WDSR* SL4 41 G2
**Addison Cl** *IVER* SL0 29 G2
**Addison Ct** *MDHD* SL6 3 J1
**Adelaide Cl** *SL* SL1 25 G4
**Adelaide Rd** *ASHF* TW15 53 H1
*WDSR* SL4 36 D5
**Adelaide Sq** *WDSR* SL4 7 G7
**Adelphi Gdns** *SL* SL1 4 C4
**Adrians Wk** *SLN* SL2 5 F2
**Agars Pl** *DTCH/LGLY* SL3 37 E3
**Aintree Cl** *DTCH/LGLY* SL3 39 G5
**Ajax Av** *SL* SL1 25 H2
**Alan Wy** *DTCH/LGLY* SL3 28 A1
**Albany Pk** *DTCH/LGLY* SL3 39 F4
**Albany Pl** *EGH* TW20 47 H5
**Albany Rd** *WDSR* SL4 7 F6
*WDSR* SL4 43 E4
**Albert Br** *DTCH/LGLY* SL3 43 F2
**Albert Cl** *SL* SL1 5 F6
**Albert Dr** *STA* TW18 52 D1
**Albert Pl** *WDSR* SL4 35 G2
**Albert Rd** *EGH* TW20 50 D2
*WDSR* SL4 42 C3
**Albert St** *MDHD* SL6 2 E5
*SL* SL1 4 E6
*WDSR* SL4 6 C5
**Albion Cl** *SLN* SL2 5 G3
**Albion Pl** *WDSR* SL4 6 A6
**Aldborough Sp** *SL* SL1 26 C1
**Aldbourne Rd** *SL* SL1 14 B5
**Aldebury Rd** *MDHD* SL6 12 A3
**Alden Vw** *WDSR* SL4 34 D5
**Alderbury Rd** *DTCH/LGLY* SL3 28 B4
**Alderbury Rd West**
*DTCH/LGLY* SL3 28 B4
**Alder Cl** *EGH* TW20 51 E1
*SL* SL1 25 F3
**Alder Rd** *IVER* SL0 19 E2
**Alderside Wk** *EGH* TW20 51 E1
**Aldin Av North** *SL* SL1 5 H4
**Aldin Av South** *SL* SL1 5 H5
**Aldridge Rd** *SLN* SL2 15 G4
**Aldwick Dr** *MDHD* SL6 2 A6
**Alexander Rd** *EGH* TW20 51 H1
**Alexandra Cl** *STA* TW18 53 H2
**Alexandra Rd** *EGH* TW20 50 C2
*MDHD* SL6 2 A3
*SL* SL1 4 B6
*WDSR* SL4 7 G7
**Alice La** *SL* SL1 14 B4
**Allenby Rd** *MDHD* SL6 21 F1
**Allerds Rd** *SLN* SL2 15 F1
**Alleyns La** *MDHD* SL6 8 D2
**All Saints Av** *MDHD* SL6 11 G5
**Allyn Cl** *STA* TW18 52 D2
**Alma Rd** *WDSR* SL4 6 E7
**Almond Cl** *EGH* TW20 50 B2
*WDSR* SL4 6 C6
**Almond Rd** *SL* SL1 14 B3
**Almons Wy** *SLN* SL2 17 F5
**Alpha St North** *SL* SL1 5 G5
**Alpha St South** *SL* SL1 5 F6
**Alpha Wy** *EGH* TW20 52 A4
**Alpine Cl** *MDHD* SL6 3 G7
**Alston Gdns** *MDHD* SL6 2 D4
**Altmore** *MDHD* SL6 20 C4
**Altona Wy** *SL* SL1 25 H1
**Alton Ct** *STA* TW18 52 C4
**Altwood Bailey** *MDHD* SL6 21 F3
**Altwood Cl** *MDHD* SL6 21 F3
*SL* SL1 15 E5
**Altwood Dr** *MDHD* SL6 21 F3
**Altwood Rd** *MDHD* SL6 21 F3
**Alvista Av** *MDHD* SL6 24 B1
**Alwyn Rd** *MDHD* SL6 11 F5
**Alyson Ct** *MDHD* SL6 * 3 F1
**Amanda Ct** *DTCH/LGLY* SL3 27 H5
**Amberley Ct** *MDHD* SL6 13
**Amberley Pl** *WDSR* SL4
**Amberley Rd** *SLN* SL2 15
**Ambleside Wy** *EGH* TW20 51
**Amerden Cl** *MDHD* SL6 23
**Amerden La** *MDHD* SL6 23
**Amerden Wy** *SL* SL1 25
**Andermans** *WDSR* SL4 * 34
**Anne Cl** *MDHD* SL6 12
**Annie Brookes Cl** *STA* TW18 48
**Ansculf Rd** *SLN* SL2 15
**Anslow Gdns** *IVER* SL0 19
**Anthony Wy** *SL* SL1 24
**Applecroft** *MDHD* SL6 21
**Appletree La** *DTCH/LGLY* SL3 27
**Approach Rd** *MDHD* SL6 23
**Arborfield Cl** *SL* SL1 4
**The Arcade** *MDHD* SL6 * 9
**Archer Cl** *MDHD* SL6 2
**The Arches** *WDSR* SL4 * 7
**Ardrossan Cl** *SLN* SL2 16
**Argent Cl** *EGH* TW20 52
**Argosy Gdns** *STA* TW18 52

La STWL/WRAY TW19 ....49 H1
v SL SL1 ....25 G2
Ct MDHD SL6 ....32 D2
ght Rd DTCH/LGLY SL3 ....45 G1
on Cl MDHD SL6 ....10 D5
ong Rd EGH TW20 ....50 C2
e Wy EGH TW20 ....51 G1
Rd STA TW18 ....53 G3
Rd SL SL1 ....4 B4
SR SL4 ....6 E4
el Cl MDHD SL6 ....11 E5
el Ct DTCH/LGLY SL3 ....37 H1
Rd MDHD SL6 ....32 B4
urne Gv MDHD SL6 ....21 G5
ok Rd WDSR SL4 ....46 B1
DTCH/LGLY SL3 ....28 D5
ft Ct SL SL1 ....14 B2
ft Rd MDHD SL6 ....11 G5
wn MDHD SL6 ....12 D2
d La MDHD SL6 ....24 B4
d Rd IVER SL0 ....19 E1
TW18 ....53 H4
STA TW18 ....53 G2
WDSR SL4 ....40 D1
gh Av EGH TW20 ....52 A3
Pk MDHD SL6 ....12 D3
n Pl MDHD SL6 ....21 E2
ood Rd EGH TW20 ....50 B2
Cl SLN SL2 ....15 H5
TW18 ....48 D4
Md WDSR SL4 ....35 E5
Cl MDHD SL6 ....3 K7
e Cl MDHD SL6 ....12 A4
e Sq WDSR SL4 ....7 F4
and Cl MDHD SL6 ....3 J3
Dr MDHD SL6 ....21 F4
Cl STA TW18 ....52 D1
t End DTCH/LGLY SL3 ....28 A1
tine Cl DTCH/LGLY SL3 ....45 G2
sgate MDHD SL6 ....10 D5
alia Av MDHD SL6 ....2 E2
alia Rd SL SL1 ....5 J4
nn Cl SL SL1 ....25 F3
nn Wk MDHD SL6 ....21 E2
ry SL SL1 ....25 G3
e Dr DTCH/LGLY SL3 ....18 B5
e Rd MDHD SL6 ....22 D3
TW18 ....52 B1
venue DTCH/LGLY SL3 ....37 F5
TW20 ....47 H5
HD SL6 ....12 D3
TW18 ....53 F4
VL/WRAY TW19 ....43 H2
SR SL4 ....43 F5
Ct SL SL1 ....24 C1
Cl SL SL1 ....25 E2
dale MDHD SL6 ....11 G4
dale Av STA TW18 ....52 D3
dale Rd ASHF TW15 ....49 H4
idges Av EGH TW20 ....52 A3
bury Crs SL SL1 ....26 B1
worth Av SLN SL2 ....15 H3
worth Sp WDSR SL4 ....46 B1
er Cl STA TW18 ....52 C4
er Dr STA TW18 ....52 C4
arth Pk MDHD SL6 ....32 D2
a Wy DTCH/LGLY SL3 ....28 A1

## B

elors Acre WDSR SL4 ....7 G5
n Cl STA TW18 ....53 E3
r Gdns SL SL1 ....25 G4
er Cl MDHD SL6 ....21 H4
Godesberg Wy MDHD SL6 ....2 E5
ninton Rd MDHD SL6 ....21 F2
hot Rd EGH TW20 ....50 C3
y Cl MDHD SL6 ....2 E4
DSR SL4 ....6 A7
Cl SL SL1 ....25 H4
ham La EGH TW20 ....50 D4
rs La MDHD SL6 ....10 D5
rs Rw MDHD SL6 * ....10 D5
win Pl MDHD SL6 ....21 G1
win Rd SL SL1 ....14 C3
win's Shore WDSR SL4 ....36 B3
rd Gn WDSR SL4 ....35 E4
oral MDHD SL6 ....11 F4
oral Cl SL SL1 ....25 E1
oral Gdns WDSR SL4 ....42 B2
bury Av SL SL1 ....15 F5
La EGH TW20 ....51 F1
gors Cl IVER SL0 ....29 H1
gors Pk IVER SL0 * ....19 G4
gors Rd North IVER SL0 ....19 F2
gors Rd South IVER SL0 ....19 G4
ks Sp SL SL1 ....25 H4
hard Rd MDHD SL6 ....21 E3
nister Cl DTCH/LGLY SL3 ....28 A4
chester Rd DTCH/LGLY SL3 ....28 B4
dney Cl MDHD SL6 ....21 H5
eman Rd MDHD SL6 ....22 A4
ey Md MDHD SL6 ....20 D3
ey Mow Rd EGH TW20 ....50 C1
n Cl MDHD SL6 ....12 B3
n Dr MDHD SL6 ....21 E4
nes Wy IVER SL0 ....29 H2
nfield IVER SL0 ....29 G1
L SL1 ....24 D3
nfield Cl MDHD SL6 ....9 F5
nway EGH TW20 ....50 C1
ons Wy EGH TW20 ....52 B2
rack La WDSR SL4 ....7 H5
r's Rd MDHD SL6 ....24 B1
ry Av WDSR SL4 ....6 D3
elotts Rd SLN SL2 ....14 D4
letts La MDHD SL6 ....32 C4
ton Rd DTCH/LGLY SL3 ....28 B4
ford Wy WDSR SL4 ....40 D2
s Md MDHD SL6 ....9 F5
es Cl DTCH/LGLY SL3 ....28 A1
n Ct MDHD SL6 ....21 G2

Bath Rd DTCH/LGLY SL3 ....39 H5
MDHD SL6 ....2 A6
MDHD SL6 ....20 B3
MDHD SL6 ....23 H1
SL SL1 ....24 D2
Bathurst Cl IVER SL0 ....29 H4
Bathurst Wk IVER SL0 ....29 G4
Battlemead Cl MDHD SL6 ....13 E2
Baxter Cl SL SL1 ....4 D6
Bayley Crs SL SL1 ....14 A5
Baylis Pde SL SL1 ....26 C1
Baylis Rd SL SL1 ....14 B4
Bay Tree Ct SL SL1 ....14 C3
Beacon Ct DTCH/LGLY SL3 ....39 E4
Beaconsfield Rd SLN SL2 ....16 A1
Beaufort Pl MDHD SL6 ....23 F4
Beauforts EGH TW20 ....50 C1
Beaulieu Cl DTCH/LGLY SL3 ....37 F5
Beaumont Cl MDHD SL6 ....21 E5
Beaumont Rd SLN SL2 ....16 B5
WDSR SL4 ....7 F7
Beckwell Rd SL SL1 ....26 A4
Bedford Av SL SL1 ....25 G1
Bedford Cl MDHD SL6 ....21 E5
Bedwins La MDHD SL6 ....8 B4
Beech Cl MDHD SL6 ....11 F5
STWL/WRAY TW19 ....49 H1
The Beeches STA TW18 * ....53 E1
Beeches Wy BNEND SL8 ....9 H2
SL SL1 ....14 B3
Beechfield Pl MDHD SL6 ....21 H4
Beech Rd DTCH/LGLY SL3 ....28 A4
Beechtree Av EGH TW20 ....50 B2
Beech Tree La STA TW18 * ....53 F5
Beechwood Av STA TW18 ....53 F2
Beechwood Dr MDHD SL6 ....21 E2
Beechwood Gdns SL SL1 ....4 D5
Beechwood Rd SLN SL2 ....16 B5
Beehive Rd STA TW18 ....52 D1
Belfast Av SL SL1 ....26 A1
Belgrave Pde SL SL1 * ....4 C1
Belgrave Rd SL SL1 ....4 E1
Bell Cl SLN SL2 ....17 F5
Belle Vue Cl STA TW18 ....53 E4
Belle Vue Pl SL SL1 * ....5 F6
Bell La WDSR SL4 ....35 F1
Bells Hl SLN SL2 ....17 E1
Bells La DTCH/LGLY SL3 ....44 D2
Bell St MDHD SL6 ....3 F6
Bellswood La IVER SL0 ....18 D5
Bell Vw WDSR SL4 ....41 F2
Bell View Cl WDSR SL4 ....41 F1
Bellweir Cl STWL/WRAY TW19 ....47 H3
Belmont SLN SL2 ....15 G5
Belmont Crs MDHD SL6 ....11 G5
Belmont Dr MDHD SL6 ....2 A2
Belmont Park Av MDHD SL6 ....2 B1
Belmont Park Rd MDHD SL6 ....2 A2
Belmont Rd MDHD SL6 ....2 C3
Belmont V MDHD SL6 ....2 A3
Bennetts Cl SL SL1 ....25 G3
Benning Cl WDSR SL4 ....40 D2
Benson Cl SLN SL2 ....5 G2
Bentley Pk SL SL1 ....14 D2
Bentley Rd SL SL1 ....25 F3
Beresford Av SLN SL2 ....27 G2
Berkeley Cl STWL/WRAY TW19 ....48 B3
Berkley Cl MDHD SL6 ....11 E5
Berkshire Av SL SL1 ....25 H1
Berners Cl SL SL1 ....25 E2
Berries Rd MDHD SL6 ....9 G3
Berry Fld SLN SL2 ....27 G1
Berry Hl MDHD SL6 ....23 F1
Berryscroft Rd STA TW18 ....53 G3
Berwick Av SL SL1 ....25 H2
Bestobell Rd SL SL1 ....26 A1
Beta Wy EGH TW20 ....52 A4
Beverley Gdns MDHD SL6 ....11 F4
Bexley St WDSR SL4 ....6 D5
Biddles Cl SL SL1 ....25 E3
Bideford Sp SLN SL2 ....15 H3
Bigfrith La MDHD SL6 ....8 A4
Billet La DTCH/LGLY SL3 ....28 D1
IVER SL0 ....18 D3
Bingham Dr STA TW18 ....53 H3
Bingham Rd SL SL1 ....14 A5
The Binghams MDHD SL6 ....22 D5
Birch Cl IVER SL0 ....19 F2
Birch Gn STA TW18 ....48 D5
Birch Gv SLN SL2 ....15 H5
WDSR SL4 ....34 D5
Birchington Rd WDSR SL4 ....6 B6
Birdwood Rd MDHD SL6 ....21 F1
Birley Rd SL SL1 ....26 B1
Bishop Ct MDHD SL6 ....2 B6
Bishops Farm Cl WDSR SL4 ....40 B1
Bishopsgate Rd WDSR SL4 ....46 A4
Bishops Orch SLN SL2 ....15 H3
Bishops Rd SL SL1 ....5 G5
Bishops Wy EGH TW20 ....52 B2
Bissley Dr MDHD SL6 ....21 E5
Bix La MDHD SL6 ....10 D4
Blackamoor La MDHD SL6 ....3 G1
Black Butt Cottages MDHD SL6 ....9 H3
Blackett Cl EGH TW20 ....52 C5
Black Horse Cl WDSR SL4 ....40 D1
Black Park Rd DTCH/LGLY SL3 ....18 B2
Blackpond La SLN SL2 ....15 H1
Blacksmith Rw DTCH/LGLY SL3 ....38 C1
Blackthorn Dell
DTCH/LGLY SL3 ....27 G5
Blackthorne Crs
DTCH/LGLY SL3 ....45 G1
Blackthorne Rd
DTCH/LGLY SL3 ....45 G2
Blair Rd SL SL1 ....4 C3
Blakeney Ct MDHD SL6 ....2 E1
Blandford Cl DTCH/LGLY SL3 ....27 H5
Blandford Rd North
DTCH/LGLY SL3 ....27 H5
Blandford Rd South
DTCH/LGLY SL3 ....27 H5
Blays Cl EGH TW20 ....50 C2
Blay's La EGH TW20 ....50 B2
Blenheim Rd DTCH/LGLY SL3 ....37 H1

MDHD SL6 ....11 F5
Blinco La DTCH/LGLY SL3 ....28 A1
Bloomfield Rd MDHD SL6 ....21 E3
Blue Ball La EGH TW20 ....51 F1
Blumfield Crs SL SL1 ....14 D5
Blunden Dr DTCH/LGLY SL3 ....38 D1
Blythe Cl IVER SL0 ....29 H1
Boadicea Cl SL SL1 ....25 E3
Boarlands Cl SL SL1 ....25 F2
Bodmin Av SLN SL2 ....15 G5
Boleyn Cl STA TW18 ....52 C1
Bolton Av WDSR SL4 ....42 B2
Bolton Crs WDSR SL4 ....42 A2
Bolton Rd WDSR SL4 ....42 A2
Bond St EGH TW20 ....50 B2
Booth Dr STA TW18 ....53 H2
Borderside SLN SL2 ....27 E1
Borrowdale Cl EGH TW20 ....51 H3
Boscombe Cl EGH TW20 ....52 A4
Boshers Gdns EGH TW20 ....51 F2
Boston Gv SL SL1 ....26 A1
Botham Dr SL SL1 ....4 C6
Boulters Cl SL SL1 ....25 G4
Boulters Ct MDHD SL6 ....13 E4
Boulters Gdns MDHD SL6 ....13 E4
Boulters La MDHD SL6 ....13 E4
Boundary Rd ASHF TW15 ....53 G1
MDHD SL6 ....13 H5
Bourne Av WDSR SL4 ....42 A3
Bourne Rd SL SL1 ....26 A4
Bouverie Wy DTCH/LGLY SL3 ....38 A2
Boveney Cl SL SL1 ....25 G4
Boveney New Rd WDSR SL4 ....35 E1
Boveney Rd WDSR SL4 ....34 C1
Bower Wy SL SL1 ....25 E2
Bowes Lyon Cl WDSR SL4 ....7 F5
Bowes Rd STA TW18 ....52 C2
Bowmans Cl SL SL1 ....14 B1
Bowry Dr STWL/WRAY TW19 ....44 B5
Bowyer Dr SL SL1 ....25 E2
Boyndon Rd MDHD SL6 ....2 B5
Boyn Hill Av MDHD SL6 ....2 B6
Boyn Hill Cl MDHD SL6 ....2 A6
Boyn Hill Rd MDHD SL6 ....21 G3
Boyn Valley Rd MDHD SL6 ....2 B7
Brackenforde DTCH/LGLY SL3 ....27 G4
Bracken Rd MDHD SL6 ....21 G4
Bradcutts La MDHD SL6 ....8 D1
Bradford Rd SL SL1 ....25 G1
Bradley Rd SL SL1 ....4 C1
Bradshaw Cl WDSR SL4 ....35 E5
Braemar Gdns SL SL1 ....25 G4
Bramber Ct SL SL1 ....25 G3
Brambledown STA TW18 ....53 F4
Bramble Dr MDHD SL6 ....21 E4
Bramley Cha MDHD SL6 ....21 G4
Bramley Cl MDHD SL6 ....21 G5
STA TW18 ....53 G2
Brammas Cl SL SL1 ....26 A5
Brampton Ct MDHD SL6 ....3 K2
Brands Rd DTCH/LGLY SL3 ....38 D3
Braybank MDHD SL6 ....23 F4
Bray Cl MDHD SL6 ....23 E5
Bray Ct MDHD SL6 ....33 E1
Brayfield Rd MDHD SL6 ....23 E4
Bray Rd MDHD SL6 ....22 D4
Braywick Rd MDHD SL6 ....3 F7
Braywood Av EGH TW20 ....51 F2
Breadcroft La MDHD SL6 ....20 D5
Breadcroft Rd MDHD SL6 ....20 D5
Bredward Cl SL SL1 ....14 B3
Bremer Rd STWL/WRAY TW19 ....49 E4
Briar Cl MDHD SL6 ....24 B1
Briar Dene MDHD SL6 ....11 G4
Briar Gln MDHD SL6 ....9 E4
The Briars DTCH/LGLY SL3 ....38 B2
Briar Wy SLN SL2 ....15 H5
Brickfield La SL SL1 ....14 A1
Bridge Av MDHD SL6 ....3 G5
MDHD SL6 ....9 E5
Bridge Cl SL SL1 ....25 F2
STA TW18 ....48 C5
Bridgeman Dr WDSR SL4 ....6 A6
Bridge Rd MDHD SL6 ....3 H4
Bridge St DTCH/LGLY SL3 ....39 F4
MDHD SL6 ....3 G4
Bridgewater Ct
DTCH/LGLY SL3 ....38 C2
Bridgewater Ter WDSR SL4 ....7 G3
Bridgewater Wy WDSR SL4 ....7 G5
Bridle Cl MDHD SL6 ....2 C1
Bridle Rd MDHD SL6 ....21 G2
Bridlington Sp SL SL1 ....25 H5
Bridport Wy SLN SL2 ....15 H4
Brighton Sp SLN SL2 ....15 H4
Brightside Av STA TW18 ....53 G3
Brill Cl MDHD SL6 ....21 H4
Bristol Wy SL SL1 ....4 E2
Britannia Wy
STWL/WRAY TW19 ....49 H1
Britwell Rd SL SL1 ....14 C3
Broadacre STA TW18 ....53 E1
Broadmark Rd SLN SL2 ....5 J1
Broad Oak SLN SL2 ....16 A4
Broad Oak Ct SLN SL2 ....16 A4
Broad Platts DTCH/LGLY SL3 ....27 H5
Broadwater Cl
STWL/WRAY TW19 ....47 E1
Broadwater Pk MDHD SL6 ....33 G2
Broadway MDHD SL6 ....3 F5
STA TW18 * ....53 F1
The Broadway STA TW18 ....53 G5
Brocas St WDSR SL4 ....7 G2
Brocas Ter WDSR SL4 ....7 G2
Brock La MDHD SL6 ....3 F5
Brockton Ct MDHD SL6 ....2 E7
Broken Furlong WDSR SL4 ....36 A2
Brompton Dr MDHD SL6 ....11 G4
Bromycroft Rd SLN SL2 ....15 G3
Brook Crs SL SL1 ....25 E1
Brookdene Cl MDHD SL6 ....12 B3
Brook Pth SL SL1 ....25 F2
Brookside DTCH/LGLY SL3 ....39 E4
Brookside Av ASHF TW15 ....53 G1
STWL/WRAY TW19 ....43 H2

Brook St WDSR SL4 ....7 H6
Broomfield Ga SLN SL2 ....15 H4
Broom Hl MDHD SL6 ....9 E4
Brownfield Gdns MDHD SL6 ....22 A3
Bruce Cl SL SL1 ....25 G3
Brudenell WDSR SL4 ....41 F2
Brunel Cl MDHD SL6 ....22 A3
Brunel Rd MDHD SL6 ....21 H3
Brunel Wy SL SL1 ....4 E3
Bryant Av SLN SL2 ....16 B5
Bryer Pl WDSR SL4 ....40 D2
Buccleuch Rd DTCH/LGLY SL3 ....37 E4
Buckingham Av SL SL1 ....25 E1
Buckingham Av East SL SL1 ....26 A1
Buckingham Gdns SL SL1 ....4 E5
Buckland Av DTCH/LGLY SL3 ....5 J7
Buckland Crs WDSR SL4 ....35 F5
Buckland Ga DTCH/LGLY SL3 ....17 F3
Bucklebury Cl MDHD SL6 ....33 E3
Budebury Rd STA TW18 ....52 D1
Buffins MDHD SL6 ....13 G3
Bulkeley Av WDSR SL4 ....41 H2
Bulkeley Cl EGH TW20 ....50 C1
Bunces Cl WDSR SL4 ....35 H2
Bundys Wy STA TW18 ....52 D2
Bunten Meade SL SL1 ....25 H3
Burchetts Green La MDHD SL6 ....20 A2
Burcot Gdns MDHD SL6 ....12 A2
Burfield Rd WDSR SL4 ....46 A1
Burford Gdns SL SL1 ....14 C5
Burges Rd STA TW18 ....53 E2
Burges Wy STA TW18 ....53 E1
Burgett Rd SL SL1 ....25 H5
Burlington Av SL SL1 ....4 C4
Burlington Rd SL SL1 ....4 D4
SL SL1 ....14 B5
Burnetts Rd WDSR SL4 ....35 E5
Burnham Cl WDSR SL4 ....40 D1
Burnham La SL SL1 ....14 D5
Burnt Oak MDHD SL6 ....9 F3
Burroway Rd DTCH/LGLY SL3 ....28 D5
Burton Wy WDSR SL4 ....41 E2
Butchers La MDHD SL6 ....30 A2
Butlers Cl WDSR SL4 ....40 D1
Buttercup Sq
STWL/WRAY TW19 * ....49 H2
Buttermere Av SL SL1 ....14 C5
Buttermere Wy EGH TW20 ....51 H3
Buxton Rd ASHF TW15 ....53 H1
Bybend Cl SLN SL2 ....15 H1
Byland Dr MDHD SL6 ....32 D2
Byron Ct WDSR SL4 ....41 G2
Byways SL SL1 ....14 A5

## C

Caddy Cl EGH TW20 ....51 G1
Cadogan Cl MDHD SL6 ....32 C3
Cadwell Dr MDHD SL6 ....21 H5
Calbroke Rd SLN SL2 ....15 F4
Calder Cl MDHD SL6 ....2 C1
Calder Ct DTCH/LGLY SL3 ....38 B2
MDHD SL6 ....2 B1
Calder Wy DTCH/LGLY SL3 ....45 G2
Callow Hl VW GU25 ....50 C5
Cambridge Av SL SL1 ....14 B2
SL SL1 ....25 G1
Camden Rd MDHD SL6 ....11 H4
Camley Gdns MDHD SL6 ....11 E5
Camley Park Dr MDHD SL6 ....10 D5
Camm Av WDSR SL4 ....41 E2
Camperdown MDHD SL6 ....3 K1
Canada Rd SL SL1 ....5 J4
Canal Est DTCH/LGLY SL3 * ....28 C4
Canal Whf DTCH/LGLY SL3 ....28 C4
Cannock Cl MDHD SL6 ....3 J7
Cannon Court Rd MDHD SL6 ....11 H3
Cannondown Rd MDHD SL6 ....9 E5
Cannon Ga SLN SL2 ....27 G2
Cannon Hill Cl MDHD SL6 ....33 E1
Cannon La MDHD SL6 ....20 D3
Canon Hill Dr MDHD SL6 ....22 D5
Canon Hill Wy MDHD SL6 ....32 D1
Canterbury Av SLN SL2 ....16 A4
Canterbury Ms WDSR SL4 ....6 C6
Cardigan Cl SL SL1 ....25 F2
Cardinals Wk MDHD SL6 ....24 C1
Carey Cl WDSR SL4 ....41 H2
Carisbrooke Cl MDHD SL6 ....21 G3
Carlisle Rd SL SL1 ....26 B2
Carlton Rd SLN SL2 ....5 K1
Carlyle Rd STA TW18 ....52 D3
Carmarthen Rd SL SL1 ....4 C1
Carrington Rd SL SL1 ....26 C2
Carter Cl WDSR SL4 ....6 A6
Castle Av DTCH/LGLY SL3 ....37 E3
Castle Ct MDHD SL6 ....2 B4
Castle Dr MDHD SL6 ....2 B4
Castle Hl MDHD SL6 ....2 C5
WDSR SL4 ....7 H4
Castle Hill Rd EGH TW20 ....46 B5
Castle Hill Ter MDHD SL6 ....2 C5
Castle Ms MDHD SL6 ....2 C5
Castle St SL SL1 ....5 F7
Castleview Rd DTCH/LGLY SL3 ....37 G1
The Causeway MDHD SL6 ....23 E4
STA TW18 ....48 B5
Cavalry Crs WDSR SL4 ....41 H2
Cavendish Cl MDHD SL6 ....24 A1
Cawcott Dr WDSR SL4 ....35 E5
Cecil Rd IVER SL0 ....29 G1
Cecil Wy SLN SL2 ....15 F4
Cedar Cha MDHD SL6 ....13 F4
Cedar Cl IVER SL0 ....19 E1
STA TW18 ....53 G5
Cedar Ct EGH TW20 ....47 G5
Cedar Dr MDHD SL6 ....9 F4
Cedars Rd MDHD SL6 ....3 H5
The Cedars SLN SL2 ....15 F3
Cedar Wy DTCH/LGLY SL3 ....38 A1
Celia Crs ASHF TW15 ....53 H2
Cell Farm Av WDSR SL4 ....43 F4

Central Dr SL SL1 ....25 F2
Centre Rd WDSR SL4 * ....34 C4
Century Rd EGH TW20 ....52 A1
Chalgrove Cl MDHD SL6 ....3 J7
Chalk Pit La SL SL1 ....14 B1
Challow Ct MDHD SL6 ....2 B1
Chalvey Gdns SL SL1 ....4 C5
Chalvey Gv SL SL1 ....25 H5
Chalvey Pk SL SL1 ....4 D5
Chalvey Rd East SL SL1 ....4 C5
Chalvey Rd West SL SL1 ....4 B5
Champney Cl DTCH/LGLY SL3 ....44 C2
Chandos Rd STA TW18 ....52 B1
Chantry Cl WDSR SL4 ....6 B4
Chapels Cl SL SL1 ....25 E3
Chapel St SL SL1 ....4 E5
Chapter Ms WDSR SL4 ....7 H3
Charlotts Pl WDSR SL4 ....7 G5
Charles Gdns SLN SL2 ....27 E1
Charles Rd STA TW18 ....53 H2
Charles St WDSR SL4 ....7 F5
Charlotte Av SLN SL2 ....26 D2
Charlton WDSR SL4 ....40 C1
Charlton Cl SL SL1 ....25 H4
Charta Rd EGH TW20 ....52 A1
Charter Cl SL SL1 * ....5 F6
Charter Pl STA TW18 ....53 E2
Charter Rd SL SL1 ....25 E2
The Chase MDHD SL6 ....11 H2
Chatfield SLN SL2 ....15 G5
Chatsworth Cl MDHD SL6 ....21 G3
Chaucer Cl WDSR SL4 ....42 B2
Chaucer Wy SL SL1 ....4 E2
Chauntry Cl MDHD SL6 ....23 E2
Chauntry Ms MDHD SL6 * ....3 K6
Chauntry Rd MDHD SL6 ....3 J6
Cheniston Gv MDHD SL6 ....20 D1
Chequers Orch IVER SL0 ....29 H1
Cherington Ga MDHD SL6 ....11 F4
The Cherries SLN SL2 ....27 G1
Cherry Av DTCH/LGLY SL3 ....27 H4
Cherry Garden La MDHD SL6 ....20 C5
Cherry Orch STA TW18 ....53 E1
Cherry Tree Av STA TW18 ....53 F2
Cherry Wy DTCH/LGLY SL3 ....45 E2
Cherrywood Av EGH TW20 ....50 B2
Chertsey La STA TW18 ....52 C1
Cherwell Cl DTCH/LGLY SL3 ....38 D3
MDHD SL6 ....3 G3
Chester Rd SL SL1 ....26 B1
Chestnut Av DTCH/LGLY SL3 ....28 A4
Chestnut Cl EGH TW20 ....50 B2
MDHD SL6 ....12 D4
Chestnut Dr EGH TW20 ....50 D2
WDSR SL4 ....41 E3
Chestnut Gv STA TW18 ....53 G2
Chestnut Manor Cl STA TW18 ....53 F1
Cheveley Gdns SL SL1 ....14 C2
Cheviot Cl MDHD SL6 ....3 J7
Cheviot Rd DTCH/LGLY SL3 ....38 C2
Chichester Ct SL SL1 ....5 J6
Chiltern Cl STA TW18 ....53 E1
Chiltern Rd MDHD SL6 ....3 K7
SL SL1 ....14 B5
Chilwick Rd SLN SL2 ....15 F4
Choke La MDHD SL6 ....11 E1
Christian Sq WDSR SL4 ....7 F5
Church Cl MDHD SL6 ....2 A6
WDSR SL4 ....7 G1
Church Dr MDHD SL6 ....23 E4
Churchfield Ms SLN SL2 ....27 F1
Church Gv DTCH/LGLY SL3 ....17 G5
Churchill Rd DTCH/LGLY SL3 ....38 B1
Church La MDHD SL6 ....23 E4
SLN SL2 ....16 D4
SLN SL2 ....17 F4
WDSR SL4 ....7 H4
Church Rd EGH TW20 ....51 G1
IVER SL0 ....19 E2
MDHD SL6 ....8 B4
MDHD SL6 ....22 D3
SLN SL2 ....16 A3
WDSR SL4 ....43 F4
Church St SL SL1 ....4 A5
SL SL1 ....4 E6
SL SL1 ....14 C4
STA TW18 ....48 C5
WDSR SL4 ....7 H4
Church Ter WDSR SL4 ....41 E1
Church Vw MDHD SL6 ....30 C3
Church Views MDHD SL6 ....2 E3
Cinnamon Cl WDSR SL4 ....35 F5
Cippenham Cl SL SL1 ....25 F2
Cippenham La SL SL1 ....25 F2
SL SL1 ....26 A4
Clandon Av EGH TW20 ....52 A3
Clappers Meadow MDHD SL6 ....12 D4
Clarefield Cl MDHD SL6 ....11 E4
Clarefield Dr MDHD SL6 ....11 E4
Clarefield Rd MDHD SL6 ....11 F4
Clare Gdns EGH TW20 ....51 G1
Claremont Rd STA TW18 ....52 B1
WDSR SL4 ....6 E6
Clarence Crs WDSR SL4 ....7 F5
Clarence Dr EGH TW20 ....46 C5
Clarence Rd WDSR SL4 ....6 B6
Clarence St EGH TW20 ....51 F2
STA TW18 ....48 C5
Clarendon Ct SLN SL2 ....27 F2
Clare Rd MDHD SL6 ....2 C7
MDHD SL6 ....24 C1
STWL/WRAY TW19 ....49 H2
Clayhall La WDSR SL4 ....42 D4
Clayton Pde DTCH/LGLY SL3 * ....28 C5
Cleares Pasture SL SL1 ....14 B3
Clements Cl SL SL1 ....5 J5
Cleve Ct WDSR SL4 ....41 F2
Cleveland Cl MDHD SL6 ....3 K7
Cleveland Dr STA TW18 ....53 F5
Clewer Av WDSR SL4 ....6 C6
Clewer Court Rd WDSR SL4 ....6 C3
Clewer Flds WDSR SL4 ....6 E4
Clewer Hill Rd WDSR SL4 ....41 E1
Clewer New Town WDSR SL4 ....6 B7
Clewer Pk WDSR SL4 ....6 B3

Clifton Cl MDHD SL6 .......22 B4
Clifton Ri WDSR SL4.......34 D5
Clifton Rd SL SL1 .......5 J3
Clive Ct SL SL1 .......4 A5
Cliveden Md MDHD SL6 .......13 E3
Cliveden Rd MDHD SL6 .......13 F5
Clivemont Rd MDHD SL6 .......2 A1
Clockhouse La East EGH TW20 .......51 H3
Clockhouse La West EGH TW20 .......51 G3
Clonmel Wy SL SL1 .......14 B3
The Close IVER SL0 .......9 J3
Close St MDHD SL6 .......24 D2
Clyde Rd STWL/WRAY TW19.......49 H2
Clyve Wy STA TW18 .......52 C4
Coalmans Wy MDHD SL6 .......24 A1
Cobb Cl DTCH/LGLY SL3 .......38 A2
Cobblers Cl SLN SL2 .......15 H2
Cobham Cl SL SL1 .......25 K5
Cockett Rd DTCH/LGLY SL3 .......28 A5
Coe Sp SL SL1 .......25 H4
Coftards SLN SL2 .......27 G1
Colenorton Crs WDSR SL4 .......35 F1
Coleridge Crs DTCH/LGLY SL3 .......39 G5
Colin Wy SL SL1 .......25 H5
College Av EGH TW20 .......51 H2
  MDHD SL6 .......2 C4
  SL SL1 .......4 C6
College Crs WDSR SL4 .......6 D7
College Gln MDHD SL6 .......2 B2
College Ri MDHD SL6 .......2 B4
College Rd MDHD SL6 .......2 B3
  SL SL1 .......25 F3
Collier Cl MDHD SL6 .......2 E1
Colnbrook By-Pass STWL/WRAY TW19 .......38 D3
Coln Ct MDHD SL6 .......3 F5
Colndale Rd DTCH/LGLY SL3.......45 G1
Colne Bank STWL/WRAY TW19.......45 E2
Colne Orch IVER SL0.......29 H1
Colne Valley Wy STWL/WRAY TW19.......48 C2
Colne Wy STWL/WRAY TW19.......48 A4
Colonial Rd SL SL1 .......15 H5
Combermere Cl WDSR SL4 .......6 C7
Comet Rd STWL/WRAY TW19.......49 H1
Commercial Rd SL SL1 .......53 E2
Common La WDSR SL4 .......34 A2
Common Rd DTCH/LGLY SL3 .......38 C1
  WDSR SL4 .......34 D1
Compton Dr MDHD SL6 .......11 E5
Concorde Ct WDSR SL4 .......6 B6
Concorde Rd MDHD SL6 .......21 H4
Concorde Wy SL SL1 .......25 K5
Conduit La DTCH/LGLY SL3 .......28 A2
Conegar Ct SL SL1 .......4 C3
Conifer La EGH TW20 .......52 A1
The Conifers MDHD SL6 .......11 E5
Conifer Wk WDSR SL4 * .......34 C4
Coningsby Cl MDHD SL6 .......21 H5
Coningsby La MDHD SL6 .......33 G5
Coniston Crs SL SL1 .......14 D2
Coniston Wy EGH TW20 .......51 H5
Connaught Cl MDHD SL6 .......12 A4
Connaught Rd SL SL1 .......5 J4
Convent Rd WDSR SL4 .......6 A7
Conway Rd MDHD SL6 .......24 D1
Cookham Dean Bottom MDHD SL6 .......8 C2
Cookham Rd MDHD SL6 .......12 A3
Coombe Hill Ct WDSR SL4 .......40 D3
Coopers Cl STA TW18.......52 C1
Coopers Hill La EGH TW20.......46 D5
Coopers Rw IVER SL0.......19 H4
Cooper Wy SL SL1 .......25 H5
Cope Ct MDHD SL6 .......21 G1
Copper Beech Cl WDSR SL4 .......34 D5
Coppermill Rd STWL/WRAY TW19.......44 D5
Coppice Dr STWL/WRAY TW19.......46 D1
Coppins La IVER SL0.......19 H5
Copse Cl SL SL1 .......19 F1
Copse Wd IVER SL0 .......19 F1
Copthorn Cl MDHD SL6 .......11 H2
Corby Cl EGH TW20 .......50 C2
Corby Dr EGH TW20 .......50 C2
Cordwalles Rd MDHD SL6 .......2 D3
Cordwallis St MDHD SL6 .......2 D2
Corfe Gdns SL SL1 .......14 B5
Corfe Pl MDHD SL6 .......21 G1
Cornwall Av SLN SL2 .......16 B2
Cornwall Cl MDHD SL6 .......12 A3
  WDSR SL4 .......35 E2
Cornwall Wy STA TW18 .......52 C2
Cornwall Rd SL SL1 .......24 A4
Coronation Av DTCH/LGLY SL3 .......28 A1
Corsair Cl STWL/WRAY TW19.......49 H1
Cotswold Cl MDHD SL6 .......3 J7
  SL SL1 .......25 H5
  STA TW18.......53 E1
Cottesbrooke Cl DTCH/LGLY SL3.......38 C5
Coulson Wy SL SL1 .......14 B5
Court Cl MDHD SL6 .......21 H3
Court Crs SL SL1 .......26 B1
Court Dr MDHD SL6 .......13 E2
Courtfield Rd MDHD SL6 .......21 G2
Courthouse Rd MDHD SL6 .......2 A1
Courtlands MDHD SL6 .......2 E7
Courtlands Av DTCH/LGLY SL3.......37 H1
Court La SL SL1 .......14 D3
  WDSR SL4 .......24 A5
Coverdale Wy SL SL1 .......15 E4
Cowper Rd SLN SL2 .......15 G4
Coxborow Cl MDHD SL6 .......9 E5
Cox Green La MDHD SL6 .......21 F5
Cox Green Rd MDHD SL6 .......21 H5
Crabtree Rd EGH TW20 .......52 A5
Craigwell Cl STA TW18.......52 C4
Cranbourne Av SL SL1 .......41 F1
Cranbourne Cl SL SL1 .......26 A5
Cranbourne Rd SL SL1 .......26 A5
Cranbrook Dr MDHD SL6 .......11 F4
Craufurd Ri MDHD SL6 .......2 D3

Crayle St SLN SL2 .......15 G3
Creden Cl SL SL1 .......2 B7
Crescent Dl MDHD SL6 * .......2 E7
Crescent Dr MDHD SL6 .......21 F5
The Crescent EGH TW20 .......51 F2
  MDHD SL6 .......2 D4
  SL SL1 .......4 C5
Cress Rd SL SL1 .......25 H4
Cresswells Md MDHD SL6 .......32 D2
Crimp Hl EGH TW20 .......46 A3
Crofters WDSR SL4 .......43 E5
The Crofters WDSR SL4 * .......43 E5
Crofthill Rd SLN SL2 .......15 H4
The Croft MDHD SL6 .......21 G3
Cross Oak WDSR SL4 .......6 A6
Crossways MDHD SL6 .......52 B2
Crosthwaite Wy SL SL1 .......14 D5
Crown Cl DTCH/LGLY SL3 .......39 E4
Crown La MDHD SL6 .......3 G4
Crown Meadow DTCH/LGLY SL3.......38 D4
Crown Sq MDHD SL6 * .......3 J4
Crown St EGH TW20 .......51 G1
Croxley Ri MDHD SL6 .......2 A7
Crummock Cl SL SL1 .......24 C1
Culham Dr MDHD SL6 .......12 A3
Cullen's Pas MDHD SL6 .......3 F5
Culley Wy MDHD SL6 .......21 G3
Cumberland Av SLN SL2 .......16 A4
Cumberland Rd ASHF TW15.......49 H4
Cumberland St STA TW18.......52 B1
Cumbrae Cl SLN SL2 .......5 H2
Cumbria Cl MDHD SL6 .......21 G4
Curfew Yd WDSR SL4 * .......7 G2
Curls La MDHD SL6 .......22 A4
Curls Rd MDHD SL6 .......21 H4
The Cygnets STA TW18.......52 D1
Cypress Wk EGH TW20.......50 B2

**D**

Dagmar Rd WDSR SL4.......7 G6
Dairy Ct MDHD SL6 .......32 C4
Daisy Meadow EGH TW20 .......51 G2
Daleham Av EGH TW20 .......51 G2
Damson Gv SL SL1 .......26 A4
Dandridge Cl DTCH/LGLY SL3 .......27 G5
Danehurst Cl EGH TW20 .......51 E2
Danes Gdns MDHD SL6 .......9 F4
Darling's La MDHD SL6 .......10 C5
Darrell Cl DTCH/LGLY SL3 .......38 B1
Dart Cl DTCH/LGLY SL3 .......38 D5
Darvill's La SL SL1 .......4 B5
Darwin Rd DTCH/LGLY SL3 .......28 B4
Dashwood Cl DTCH/LGLY SL3 .......37 G1
Datchet Pl DTCH/LGLY SL3 .......37 F5
Datchet Rd DTCH/LGLY SL3 .......44 B2
  WDSR SL4 .......7 J1
  SL4 .......43 E4
Daventry Cl DTCH/LGLY SL3 .......39 H5
David Rd DTCH/LGLY SL3 .......45 H1
Dawes East Rd SL SL1 .......14 C4
Dawes Moor Cl SLN SL2 .......27 G1
Dawley Ride DTCH/LGLY SL3 .......39 G5
Dawn Redwood Cl DTCH/LGLY SL3 .......44 C2
Dawson Cl WDSR SL4 .......6 A6
Deal Av SL SL1 .......15 E5
Dean Cl WDSR SL4 .......40 D2
Dean La MDHD SL6 .......8 B2
Deans Cl SLN SL2 .......17 F1
Deansfield Cl MDHD SL6 .......11 G3
Dean Vw MDHD SL6 .......9 E4
Decies Wy SL SL1 .......17 E1
Dedworth Dr WDSR SL4 .......35 E5
Dedworth Rd WDSR SL4 .......6 A6
Deena Cl SL SL1 .......25 E2
Deep Fld DTCH/LGLY SL3 .......37 F4
Dee Rd WDSR SL4 * .......34 C4
Deerswood MDHD SL6 .......3 H1
Delaford Cl IVER SL0 * .......29 H1
The Dell MDHD SL6 * .......20 D5
Delta Wy EGH TW20 .......52 A4
Denham Cl MDHD SL6 .......21 G2
Denham Rd EGH TW20 .......47 G5
Denmark St MDHD SL6 .......19 F1
Dennis Wy SL SL1 .......2 D2
Denny Rd DTCH/LGLY SL3 .......24 D2
Derek Rd MDHD SL6 .......38 B1
De Ros Pl EGH TW20 .......13 E5
Derwent Dr MDHD SL6 .......51 G2
Derwent Rd MDHD SL6 .......12 A2
Desborough Crs MDHD SL6 .......14 C5
Deseronto St DTCH/LGLY SL3 * .......21 G3
Devereux Rd WDSR SL4 .......28 A4
Deverills Wy DTCH/LGLY SL3 .......7 G6
Devil's La EGH TW20 .......39 E1
Devon Av SL SL1 .......52 A2
Devonshire Gn SLN SL2 .......26 A1
Dhoon Ri MDHD SL6 .......15 H2
Diamedes Av STWL/WRAY TW19.......3 F7
Diamond Rd SL SL1 .......49 H1
Diana Cl DTCH/LGLY SL3 .......5 H4
Dickens Pl DTCH/LGLY SL3 .......28 A1
Ditton Maze MDHD SL6 .......39 G5
Ditton Park Rd DTCH/LGLY SL3 .......11 E4
Ditton Rd DTCH/LGLY SL3 .......38 A3
Doddsfield Rd SLN SL2 .......37 H5
Dolphin Ct SL SL1 .......15 G3
Dolphin Ct North STWL/WRAY TW19 * .......5 K5
Dolphin Rd SL SL1 .......49 E4
Donnington Gdns MDHD SL6 .......2 E1

Dorchester Cl MDHD SL6 .......11 F4
Dornels SLN SL2 .......27 G1
Dorney Reach Rd MDHD SL6 .......23 H5
Dorney Wood Rd SL SL1 .......14 C1
Dorset Rd ASHF TW15.......49 H5
  SL SL1 .......7 F6
Douglas La STWL/WRAY TW19.......44 A4
Douglas Rd SLN SL2 .......16 B5
The Doultons STA TW18.......52 C1
Dove House Crs SLN SL2 .......15 E3
Dover Rd SL SL1 .......25 F1
Dower Pk WDSR SL4 .......41 E3
Down Pl WDSR SL4 .......34 A3
Downs Rd DTCH/LGLY SL3 .......37 H1
Drake Av DTCH/LGLY SL3 .......37 H1
  STA TW18.......52 D1
Drift Wy DTCH/LGLY SL3 .......39 E5
The Drive DTCH/LGLY SL3 .......28 A4
  DTCH/LGLY SL3 .......37 F5
  MDHD SL6 * .......3 J4
  STWL/WRAY TW19.......43 H5
Dropmore Rd SL SL1 .......14 C2
Drummond Cl SL SL1 .......26 A5
Dudley Wnf IVER SL0 * .......29 E3
Duffield Rd SL SL1 .......16 D5
Duke St WDSR SL4 .......6 E4
Dunbar Cl SLN SL2 .......27 E2
Duncan Gdns STA TW18.......53 E2
Duncannon Crs WDSR SL4 .......40 D2
Duncroft WDSR SL4 .......41 F2
Dundee Rd SL SL1 .......25 H1
Dungrove Hill La MDHD SL6 .......10 A2
Dunholme End MDHD SL6 .......21 H5
Dunster Gdns SL SL1 .......25 G1
Dupre Cl SL SL1 .......24 A4
Durham Av SL SL1 .......25 G1
Dutton Wy IVER SL0 .......29 H1
Dyson Cl WDSR SL4 .......41 F1

**E**

Earlsfield MDHD SL6 .......33 E1
Earls La SL SL1 .......25 F3
Eastbourne Rd SL SL1 .......25 H4
Eastbridge SLN SL2 * .......5 K3
East Burnham La SLN SL2 .......15 G1
East Crs WDSR SL4 .......35 H5
Eastcroft SLN SL2 .......15 H4
Eastfield Cl SL SL1 * .......5 G6
Eastfield Rd SL SL1 .......14 A5
East Stanley Gn DTCH/LGLY SL3 .......38 B1
Ebsworth Cl MDHD SL6 .......13 E3
Eden Cl DTCH/LGLY SL3 .......45 H1
Edgell Rd STA TW18.......52 D2
Edinburgh Av SL SL1 .......25 G1
Edinburgh Dr STA TW18.......53 G1
Edinburgh Gdns WDSR SL4 .......7 H7
Edinburgh Rd MDHD SL6 .......12 A4
Edith Rd MDHD SL6 .......21 E1
Edmunds Wy SL SL1 .......17 F5
Edward Ct STA TW18.......53 G2
  SL SL1 .......4 C5
Egerton Rd SLN SL2 .......15 E4
Egham By-Pass EGH TW20 .......51 E1
Egham Rd WDSR SL4 .......47 F5
Egham Wy EGH TW20 .......50 D2
Egremont Gdns SL SL1 .......25 G3
Eight Acres SL SL1 .......14 B4
Elbow Meadow DTCH/LGLY SL3 * .......39 H5
Elder Wy DTCH/LGLY SL3 * .......28 B4
Elizabethan Wy STWL/WRAY TW19.......49 H1
Elizabeth Av STA TW18.......53 G2
Elizabeth Wy SLN SL2 .......16 D1
Elliman Av SL SL1 .......26 C2
Ellington Ct MDHD SL6 .......23 E1
Ellington Gdns MDHD SL6 .......23 E1
Ellington Pk MDHD SL6 .......2 D1
Ellington Rd MDHD SL6 .......23 E1
Ellis Av SL SL1 .......4 C4
Ellison Cl WDSR SL4 .......41 F2
Elmar Gn SLN SL2 .......15 G3
Embank Av EGH TW20 .......50 B3
Elm Cl STWL/WRAY TW19.......49 H2
Elm Cft DTCH/LGLY SL3 .......37 G5
Elm Gv MDHD SL6 .......2 D4
Emhurst Rd DTCH/LGLY SL3 .......37 G5
Elm Rd WDSR SL4 .......41 H2
Elmshott La SL SL1 .......25 E2
Elmsleigh Rd STA TW18.......52 D1
Elmwood MDHD SL6 .......12 D1
Elmwood Rd SLN SL2 .......5 K4
Eltham Av SL SL1 .......25 E4
Elton Dr MDHD SL6 .......2 E2
Elwell Cl EGH TW20 .......51 G2
Ely Av SL SL1 .......16 A5
The Embankment STWL/WRAY TW19.......46 C1
Ember Rd DTCH/LGLY SL3 .......28 D5
Emerald Ct SL SL1 .......4 D5
Englefield Cl EGH TW20 .......50 C2
Englehurst EGH TW20 .......50 C2
English Gdns STWL/WRAY TW19.......43 H5
Ennerdale Crs SL SL1 .......24 C1
Ensign Cl STWL/WRAY TW19.......49 H2
Ensign Wy STWL/WRAY TW19.......49 H2
Erica Cl SL SL1 .......25 E2
Errington Dr WDSR SL4 .......6 B6
Eskdale Gdns MDHD SL6 .......32 D1
Essex Av SL SL1 .......25 E1
Eton Cl DTCH/LGLY SL3 .......37 E3
Eton Ct STA TW18.......52 D1
  WDSR SL4 .......7 G2
Eton Rd DTCH/LGLY SL3 .......37 E3
Eton Sq WDSR SL4 .......7 F3
Eton Wick Rd WDSR SL4 .......35 E4
Evenlode MDHD SL6 .......3 K6
Everard Av SL SL1 .......4 C4
Everest Rd STWL/WRAY TW19.......49 H1
Evergreen Ct STWL/WRAY TW19 * .......49 H1
Evergreen Oak Av WDSR SL4 .......43 E2

Evergreen Wy STWL/WRAY TW19.......49 H1
Eversley Wy EGH TW20.......52 A5
Evreham Rd IVER SL0 .......29 G1

**F**

Fairacre MDHD SL6 .......21 G2
Faircroft SLN SL2 .......15 H4
Fairfield Ap STWL/WRAY TW19 .......43 H5
Fairfield Av DTCH/LGLY SL3 .......37 G4
  STA TW18.......48 D5
Fairfield La SLN SL2 .......15 H2
Fairfield Rd SL SL1 .......14 C3
  STWL/WRAY TW19.......43 H5
Fairford Rd MDHD SL6 .......21 H5
Fairhaven EGH TW20 .......51 F1
Fairham Pk WDSR SL4 .......41 E3
Fairlawns SL SL1 .......53 F2
Fairlea MDHD SL6 .......21 E4
Fairlie Rd SL SL1 .......25 G1
Fairlight Av WDSR SL4 .......24 A1
Fairview Rd MDHD SL6 .......15 F4
  SLN SL2 .......15 F4
The Fairway MDHD SL6 .......21 F5
  SL SL1 .......14 C3
Falaise EGH TW20 .......51 E1
Falconwood EGH TW20 .......51 E1
The Fallows MDHD SL6 * .......3 H1
Falmouth Rd SL SL1 .......25 G1
Fane Wy MDHD SL6 .......21 G2
Faraday Cl SLN SL2 * .......15 H5
Faraday Rd SLN SL2 .......15 H5
Farnham Rd SL SL1 .......24 D4
The Farthingales MDHD SL6 .......3 J5
Farthing Green La SLN SL2 .......17 E2
Fawcett Rd WDSR SL4 .......6 D5
Fawley Cl MDHD SL6 .......11 H5
Fawsley Cl DTCH/LGLY SL3 .......39 G4
Feathers La STWL/WRAY TW19.......47 G5
Fenton Av STA TW18.......53 G2
Ferndale Pk MDHD SL6 .......32 C2
Ferndale Rd ASHF TW15.......53 H1
Fern Dr MDHD SL6 .......24 B1
The Fernery STA TW18.......52 C1
Fernleigh MDHD SL6 * .......3 J7
Fernley Ct MDHD SL6 .......20 D4
Fern Wk ASHF TW15.......53 H1
Ferrers Cl SL SL1 .......25 E3
Ferry Av STA TW18.......52 C5
Ferry End MDHD SL6 .......23 E4
Ferry La MDHD SL6 .......9 J3
  STWL/WRAY TW19.......47 H5
Ferry Rd MDHD SL6 .......23 E4
Ferryside MDHD SL6 .......23 E4
Fetty Pl MDHD SL6 .......21 H4
Field Hurst DTCH/LGLY SL3 .......38 B5
Fielding Gdns DTCH/LGLY SL3 .......27 G4
Fielding Rd MDHD SL6 .......21 H1
The Fieldings MDHD SL6 .......32 B4
Field Vw EGH TW20 .......52 A1
Fifield Rd MDHD SL6 .......33 F5
Filey Sp SL SL1 .......25 H5
Filmer Rd WDSR SL4 .......40 D1
Finch Ct MDHD SL6 .......21 G1
Firbank Pl EGH TW20 .......50 B2
Firs Av WDSR SL4 .......41 F2
Firs Dr DTCH/LGLY SL3 .......28 B3
Firs La MDHD SL6 .......20 D4
First Crs SL SL1 .......16 A5
Fir Tree Av SLN SL2 .......15 H2
Fishery Rd MDHD SL6 .......2 E5
Fishguard Sp SL SL1 .......15 H5
Fitzrobert Pl EGH TW20 .......51 G2
Flamborough Sp SL SL1 .......25 H5
Fleetwood Rd SL SL1 .......5 F2
Florence Cl SL SL1 .......15 K4
Florence Gdns STA TW18.......53 F5
Follejohn Wy MDHD SL6 .......30 D2
Follett Cl WDSR SL4 .......43 E5
Fontwell Cl MDHD SL6 .......10 D5
Forest Pk WDSR SL4 .......41 E5
Forest Rd WDSR SL4 .......40 D1
Forlease Cl MDHD SL6 .......3 H6
Forlease Dr MDHD SL6 .......3 H6
Forlease Rd MDHD SL6 .......3 H6
Fords Cl DTCH/LGLY SL3 .......37 H1
Foster Av WDSR SL4 .......40 D1
Fosters Pth SLN SL2 .......15 F4
Fotheringay Gdns SL SL1 .......25 G2
Foundry La DTCH/LGLY SL3 .......45 H1
Fountain Gdns WDSR SL4 .......42 D2
Foxborough Cl DTCH/LGLY SL3 .......38 C2
Foxborough Ct MDHD SL6 .......32 B4
Foxglove Cl STWL/WRAY TW19.......49 H2
Fox Rd DTCH/LGLY SL3 .......37 H1
Frances Av MDHD SL6 .......13 E4
Frances Rd WDSR SL4 .......7 F4
Francis Wy SL SL1 .......24 D2
Franklin Av SLN SL2 .......15 H5
Franklyn Crs WDSR SL4 .......40 D2

Frank Sutton Wy SL SL1 .......
Frascati Wy MDHD SL6 .......
Freestone Yd DTCH/LGLY SL3 * .......3
Frenchum Gdns SL SL1 .......25
Friary Rd STWL/WRAY TW19.......43
The Friary STWL/WRAY TW19.......2
The Frithe SLN SL2 .......2
Frogmore Cl SL SL1 .......2
Frogmore Dr WDSR SL4 .......3
Frymley Vw WDSR SL4 .......3
Fullbrook Cl MDHD SL6 .......
Furness WDSR SL4 .......40
Furnival Av SLN SL2 .......1
Furrow Wy MDHD SL6 .......2
Furzedown Cl EGH TW20 .......5
Furzen Cl SL SL1 .......1
Furze Platt Rd MDHD SL6 .......1
Furze Rd MDHD SL6 .......2
Fuzzens Wk WDSR SL4 .......4

**G**

Gables Cl DTCH/LGLY SL3 .......3
  MDHD SL6 .......
Gage Cl MDHD SL6 .......2
Gainsborough MDHD SL6 .......
Gainsborough Dr MDHD SL6 .......2
Galahad Cl SL SL1 .......
Galleons La DTCH/LGLY SL3 .......17
Galleymead Rd DTCH/LGLY SL3 .......3
Galloway Cha SLN SL2 .......
Gallys Rd WDSR SL4 .......3
Galvin Rd SL SL1 .......
Garden Cl MDHD SL6 .......
Gardner House MDHD SL6 * .......1
Gardner Rd MDHD SL6 .......
Garfield Pl WDSR SL4 .......
Garnet Cl SL SL1 .......2
George Green Rd SLN SL2 .......1
Garrick Ct STA TW18.......5
Garson La STWL/WRAY TW19.......
Garthlands MDHD SL6 .......1
Gascon's Gv SLN SL2 .......1
Gas La MDHD SL6 .......
Gatehouse Cl WDSR SL4 .......4
Gatewick Cl SL SL1 .......
Gatward Av MDHD SL6 .......2
Gaveston Rd SLN SL2 .......
George Green Dr DTCH/LGLY SL3 .......
George Green Rd DTCH/LGLY SL3 .......2
George St STA TW18.......4
Georgian Cl STA TW18.......4
Gervaise Cl SL SL1 .......2
Gibraltar La MDHD SL6 .......
Gibson Ct DTCH/LGLY SL3 .......38
Gilliat Rd SL SL1 .......
Gilliatt Ct IVER SL0 .......2
Gilman Crs WDSR SL4 .......4
Gilmore Cl SLN SL2 .......1
Gilson Ct STWL/WRAY TW19.......4
The Glade STA TW18.......5
Gladstone Wy SL SL1 .......
Glaisyer Wy IVER SL0 .......1
Glanmor Rd SLN SL2 .......
The Glanty EGH TW20 .......5
Glasgow Rd SL SL1 .......2
Glazebrook Ct MDHD SL6 .......2
Glebe Rd EGH TW20 .......5
  MDHD SL6 .......2
  STA TW18.......53
  WDSR SL4 .......
Glenavon Gdns DTCH/LGLY SL3 .......3
The Glen DTCH/LGLY SL3 .......3
  MDHD SL6 * .......
Glentworth Pl SL SL1 .......2
Gloucester Av SL SL1 .......1
Gloucester Crs STA TW18.......5
Gloucester Dr STWL/WRAY TW19.......4
Gloucester Pl WDSR SL4 .......4
Gloucester Rd MDHD SL6 .......12
Godolphin Rd SL SL1 .......2
Golden Ball La MDHD SL6 .......10
Goldsworthy Wy SL SL1 .......1
Goodman Pk SLN SL2 .......2
Goodwin Rd SL SL1 .......1
Goose Gn SLN SL2 .......1
Gordon Cl STA TW18.......53
Gordon Rd MDHD SL6 .......
  WDSR SL4 .......4
Gore Rd SL SL1 .......
Goring Rd STA TW18.......5
Gorse Meade SL SL1 .......2
Gorse Rd MDHD SL6 .......2
Goslar Wy WDSR SL4 .......
Gosling Gn DTCH/LGLY SL3 .......2
Gosling Rd DTCH/LGLY SL3 .......28
Goswell Rd WDSR SL4 .......
Gowings Gn SL SL1 .......2
Grace Ct SL SL1 .......
Grafton Cl DTCH/LGLY SL3 .......
  MDHD SL6 .......2
Graham Cl MDHD SL6 .......21
Graham Rd MDHD SL6 .......1
Grampian Wy DTCH/LGLY SL3 .......38
Grand Union Canal Wk DTCH/LGLY SL3 .......2
  SLN SL2 .......
Grange Cl STWL/WRAY TW19.......44
Grange Ct EGH TW20 .......51
Grange La MDHD SL6 .......5
Grange Rd EGH TW20 .......51
  MDHD SL6 .......5
The Grange SL SL1 * .......1
  SL SL1 .......
Grange Wy IVER SL0 .......2
Grangewood DTCH/LGLY SL3 .......1
Grant Av SL SL1 .......2
Granville Av SLN SL2 .......1

olm Wy DTCH/LGLY SL3 39 E1
nere Av SLN SL2 5 G1
nere Cl EGH TW20 51 H3
nere Pde SLN SL2 * 27 F2
y La MDHD SL6 2 C4
on Dr WDSR SL4 41 E3
Park Rd SLN SL2 17 E2
Pl SLN SL2 5 F2
Rd SL SL1 4 E2
Hill Crs MDHD SL6 21 F3
acre WDSR SL4 41 E1
acre Ct EGH TW20 * 50 C2
Cl MDHD SL6 3 F1
DHD SL6 24 A1
ndale Ms SLN SL2 5 G1
ne Fielde End STA TW18 53 H3
nfern Av SL SL1 24 C1
nfields MDHD SL6 3 G7
nlake Ter STA TW18 * 53 E3
nlands Rd STA TW18 49 E5
n La DTCH/LGLY SL3 37 F5
H TW20 47 H5
H TW20 52 A5
DHD SL6 22 D4
SL1 14 C3
DSR SL4 6 C6
n Lane Ct SL SL1 14 C3
nleaf Ct DTCH/LGLY SL3 37 E3
n Leys MDHD SL6 12 B3
nock Rd SL SL1 25 G1
n Pk STA TW18 48 C4
nside SLN SL2 15 G5
Green ASHF TW15 * 53 H1
H TW20 46 C5
SL1 4 A5
WL/WRAY TW19 44 A5
n Wy SL SL1 14 B2
nway Dr STA TW18 53 G4
nways EGH TW20 51 E2
nways Dr MDHD SL6 11 E5
Greenway SL SL1 24 D3
ory Dr WDSR SL4 43 F5
fell Av MDHD SL6 2 E6
fell Pl MDHD SL6 2 E6
fell Rd MDHD SL6 2 C5
ville Cl SL SL1 14 B2
ham Rd SL SL1 25 G1
TA TW18 52 D1
stoke Rd SLN SL2 15 F5
in Cl MDHD SL6 22 A3
SL1 26 A4
ger Hl MDHD SL6 2 B2
venor Dr MDHD SL6 13 E5
venor Rd STA TW18 53 E3
e Cl SL SL1 5 F6
DSR SL4 46 B1
e Ct EGH TW20 51 G1
e Rd MDHD SL6 3 F5
DSR SL4 7 H6
es Wy MDHD SL6 9 E4
Grove EGH TW20 51 G1
SL1 5 G5
wood La MDHD SL6 8 A3
rds Club Rd MDHD SL6 23 E1
rds Rd WDSR SL4 40 C1
dford St STA TW18 53 E2
ndale MDHD SL6 11 G4
ent Cl MDHD SL6 21 F4
nne Cl WDSR SL4 35 E5


# H


don Rd MDHD SL6 21 G3
low Ct SL SL1 26 A3
rian Wy STWL/WRAY TW19 49 H1
Hill La MDHD SL6 24 A1
g Dr SL SL1 25 H4
e St STA TW18 48 C5
fax Cl MDHD SL6 11 E5
fax Rd MDHD SL6 11 E5
fax Wy MDHD SL6 11 E5
kingcroft DTCH/LGLY SL3 27 G4
Ct DTCH/LGLY SL3 37 F4
dore Hl MDHD SL6 9 E3
Meadow SL SL1 14 C2
nbleton STWL/WRAY TW19 * 46 C2
nilton Gdns SL SL1 14 B3
nilton Pk MDHD SL6 21 E2
nilton Rd SL SL1 25 G1
n La EGH TW20 46 B5
WDSR SL4 43 G3
npden Cl SLN SL2 17 E3
npden Rd DTCH/LGLY SL3 28 B5
MDHD SL6 11 F5
npshire Av SL SL1 16 A5
nbury Cl SL SL1 14 A5
nley Cl WDSR SL4 34 D5
nover Cl EGH TW20 50 B2
SL SL1 5 G6
WDSR SL4 35 F5
nover Ga SL SL1 25 F3
nover Md MDHD SL6 23 E5
nover Wy WDSR SL4 41 F1
rcourt STWL/WRAY TW19 44 A5
rcourt Cl EGH TW20 52 A2
MDHD SL6 23 H5
rcourt Rd MDHD SL6 23 H5
WDSR SL4 35 E5
rdell Cl EGH TW20 51 G1
rdings Rw IVER SL0 19 E3
rdwick Cl MDHD SL6 10 D5
rdy Cl SL SL1 25 G3
refield Rd MDHD SL6 21 E1
re Shoots MDHD SL6 22 A3
rewood Pl SL SL1 5 H6
rgrave Rd MDHD SL6 2 B2
rkness Rd SL SL1 14 B5
rrington Cl WDSR SL4 41 F3
rris Gdns SL SL1 26 A4
rrison Wy SL SL1 24 D3
rrogate Ct DTCH/LGLY SL3 38 C2
rrow Cl MDHD SL6 12 A4
Harrow La MDHD SL6 2 B1
Harrow Rd DTCH/LGLY SL3 28 B5
Hartland Cl SL SL1 4 A3
Hartley Cl DTCH/LGLY SL3 17 G1
Hartley Copse WDSR SL4 43 E5
Harvest Hill Rd MDHD SL6 22 A4
Harvest Rd EGH TW20 50 D1
Harvey Rd DTCH/LGLY SL3 28 D5
Harwich Rd SL SL1 25 G1
Harwood Gdns WDSR SL4 46 B1
Haslemere Rd WDSR SL4 6 A5
Hasting Cl MDHD SL6 33 E1
Hastings Meadow SLN SL2 * 17 E1
Hatchgate Gdns SL SL1 14 D3
Hatch La WDSR SL4 41 G2
The Hatch WDSR SL4 34 C4
Hatfield Cl MDHD SL6 21 G2
Hatfield Rd SL SL1 5 G5
Hatton Av SLN SL2 16 B4
Hatton Ct WDSR SL4 6 E7
Havelock Crs MDHD SL6 21 F1
Havelock Rd MDHD SL6 21 F1
Hawkshill Rd SLN SL2 15 G3
Hawksway STA TW18 48 D4
Hawthorn Cl IVER SL0 19 E3
Hawthorne Ct
STWL/WRAY TW19 * 49 H1
Hawthorne Crs SL SL1 26 C1
Hawthorne Rd STA TW18 52 A1
Hawthorn Gdns MDHD SL6 21 H3
The Hawthorns DTCH/LGLY SL3 39 H5
Hawtrey Cl SL SL1 5 K5
Hawtrey Rd WDSR SL4 6 E6
Haymill Rd SL SL1 14 D4
Haynes Cl DTCH/LGLY SL3 38 B2
Hayse Hl WDSR SL4 34 D5
Haywards Md WDSR SL4 35 F2
Hazel Cl EGH TW20 50 B2
Hazel Gv STA TW18 53 F2
Hazelhurst Rd SL SL1 14 C2
Hazell Cl MDHD SL6 3 F2
Hazlemere Rd SLN SL2 5 K2
Headington Cl MDHD SL6 21 E1
Headington Rd MDHD SL6 11 E5
Hearne Dr MDHD SL6 32 C3
Heathcote MDHD SL6 32 D1
Heatherden Gn IVER SL0 19 E1
Heathlands Dr MDHD SL6 21 E2
Heath Wy IVER SL0 19 F2
Hedingham Ms MDHD SL6 * 2 A5
Helena Rd WDSR SL4 7 G6
Helston La WDSR SL4 6 C5
Helvellyn Cl EGH TW20 51 H3
Hemming Wy SLN SL2 15 H3
Hempson Av DTCH/LGLY SL3 27 G5
Hemsdale MDHD SL6 11 F4
Hemwood Rd WDSR SL4 40 D2
Hencroft St North SL SL1 5 F5
Hencroft St South SL SL1 5 F6
Hendons Wy MDHD SL6 32 D2
Hengrove Crs ASHF TW15 49 H4
Henley Rd MDHD SL6 10 B5
SL SL1 25 E1
Henry Rd SL SL1 4 B4
Hensworth Rd ASHF TW15 53 H2
Hereford Cl STA TW18 53 F4
Heritage Ct EGH TW20 51 F1
Hermitage Cl DTCH/LGLY SL3 27 G5
Hermitage La WDSR SL4 41 G2
Herndon Cl EGH TW20 47 G5
Heron Dr DTCH/LGLY SL3 38 D1
Heronfield EGH TW20 50 B2
Herschel Park Dr SL SL1 4 E5
Herschel St SL SL1 4 E5
Hetherington Cl SLN SL2 15 F3
Hever Cl MDHD SL6 21 G2
Heynes Gn MDHD SL6 21 F5
Heywood Av MDHD SL6 31 E2
Heywood Court Cl MDHD SL6 31 E2
Hibbert Rd MDHD SL6 22 D4
Highfield Ct EGH TW20 50 C2
Highfield La MDHD SL6 21 E4
Highfield Rd EGH TW20 50 D2
MDHD SL6 21 F1
WDSR SL4 41 F2
Highgrove Pk MDHD SL6 2 C2
High Rd MDHD SL6 9 E3
High St DTCH/LGLY SL3 37 F5
DTCH/LGLY SL3 38 C1
DTCH/LGLY SL3 39 E4
EGH TW20 51 G1
IVER SL0 29 H1
MDHD SL6 2 E5
MDHD SL6 9 G3
MDHD SL6 13 G4
MDHD SL6 23 E4
SL SL1 4 A6
SL SL1 4 D4
SL SL1 14 C3
STA TW18 48 D5
STWL/WRAY TW19 44 A5
WDSR SL4 7 H4
High Town Rd MDHD SL6 2 E5
Highway Av MDHD SL6 21 E1
Highway Rd MDHD SL6 21 F2
Hillary Rd DTCH/LGLY SL3 28 A5
Hillcrest Av MDHD SL6 9 E5
Hillersdon SLN SL2 17 F5
Hill Farm Rd MDHD SL6 13 G3
Hillmead Ct MDHD SL6 13 H5
Hillrise DTCH/LGLY SL3 38 C3
Hill Side MDHD SL6 * 9 F3
Hillside MDHD SL6 21 H3
SL SL1 4 C5
Hills La MDHD SL6 8 C3
Hill View Rd STWL/WRAY
TW19 43 H5
Hilperton Rd SL SL1 4 C4
Hindhay La MDHD SL6 11 F2
Hinksey Cl DTCH/LGLY SL3 28 D5
Hinton Rd SL SL1 25 E2
Hitcham La SL SL1 14 A3
Hitcham Rd SL SL1 14 A4
Hobbis Dr MDHD SL6 21 E2
Hodge La WDSR SL4 * 42 A3
Hogarth Cl SL SL1 25 E2
Hogfair La SL SL1 14 C4
Holbrook Meadow
EGH TW20 52 A2
Holland Gdns EGH TW20 52 D5
Hollow Hill La IVER SL0 28 D2
Hollybush La IVER SL0 28 D1
MDHD SL6 8 B4
Holly Cl EGH TW20 50 B2
Hollycombe EGH TW20 46 D5
Holly Crs WDSR SL4 40 D1
Holly Dr MDHD SL6 3 F2
WDSR SL4 42 C4
Holmanleaze MDHD SL6 3 G4
Holmdale SLN SL2 27 G2
Holmlea Rd DTCH/LGLY SL3 37 H5
Holmlea Wk DTCH/LGLY SL3 37 G5
Holmsdale Cl IVER SL0 29 H1
Holmwood Cl MDHD SL6 21 F3
Holyport Rd MDHD SL6 32 D3
Holyport St MDHD SL6 32 C3
Home Farm Wy
DTCH/LGLY SL3 17 G1
Home Meadow SLN SL2 16 A2
Homers Rd WDSR SL4 34 D5
Homeside Cl MDHD SL6 12 A3
Homestead Rd MDHD SL6 21 H4
STA TW18 53 F2
Homewood DTCH/LGLY SL3 27 H1
Honeysuckle Cl IVER SL0 29 E1
Honnor Rd STA TW18 53 H3
Hornbeam Gdns SL SL1 5 G7
Horseguards Dr MDHD SL6 3 K5
Horsemoor Cl DTCH/LGLY SL3 38 C1
Horton Cl MDHD SL6 13 E4
Horton Gdns DTCH/LGLY SL3 * 44 B2
Horton Rd DTCH/LGLY SL3 37 G5
DTCH/LGLY SL3 38 D5
DTCH/LGLY SL3 44 A1
DTCH/LGLY SL3 45 G2
Howard Av SLN SL2 16 B5
Howarth Rd MDHD SL6 3 H6
Hubert Rd DTCH/LGLY SL3 27 H5
Hughenden Cl MDHD SL6 21 G2
Hughenden Rd SL SL1 26 B1
Hull Cl SL SL1 26 A4
Humber Wy DTCH/LGLY
SL3 38 C1
Hummer Rd EGH TW20 47 G5
Hungerford Av SLN SL2 16 C5
Hungerford Dr MDHD SL6 12 A2
Hunstanton Cl DTCH/LGLY SL3 39 E4
Huntercombe Cl MDHD SL6 24 B1
Huntercombe La North
SL SL1 14 C5
Huntercombe La South
MDHD SL6 24 B3
Hunters Wy SL SL1 25 E4
Huntingfield Wy EGH TW20 52 B3
Huntington Pl DTCH/LGLY SL3 28 D5
Hunt's La MDHD SL6 13 G2
Hurstdene Av STA TW18 53 F2
Hurstfield Dr MDHD SL6 24 B1
Hurst Rd SL SL1 14 D5
Hurworth Av DTCH/LGLY SL3 27 G5
Huxtable Gdns MDHD SL6 33 F3
The Hyde MDHD SL6 * 3 F2
Hylle Cl WDSR SL4 35 E5
Hythe End Rd
STWL/WRAY TW19 47 G3
Hythe Field Av EGH TW20 52 B2
Hythe Park Rd EGH TW20 52 A1
Hythe Rd STA TW18 52 B1
The Hythe STA TW18 52 C1


# I


Ilchester Cl MDHD SL6 21 G3
Ilex Cl EGH TW20 50 B3
Illingworth WDSR SL4 41 E2
Imperial Ct WDSR SL4 41 G2
Imperial Rd WDSR SL4 41 G2
India Rd SL SL1 5 J4
Ingleside DTCH/LGLY SL3 39 G5
Inkerman Rd WDSR SL4 35 F1
Innings La MDHD SL6 30 B4
Institute Rd MDHD SL6 23 H1
In The Ray MDHD SL6 3 K2
Inwood Cl MDHD SL6 8 B4
Iona Crs SL SL1 25 E1
Ipswich Rd SL SL1 25 F1
Island Cl STA TW18 48 C5
Islet Pk MDHD SL6 13 E2
Islet Park Dr MDHD SL6 13 E2
Islet Rd MDHD SL6 12 D2
Ismay Cl SL SL1 * 26 C1
Iverdale Cl IVER SL0 29 E2
Iver Ldg IVER SL0 19 H5
Ives Rd DTCH/LGLY SL3 28 C5
Ivy Cl MDHD SL6 32 C4
Ivy Crs SL SL1 25 F2


# J


Jacob Cl WDSR SL4 35 E5
James St WDSR SL4 7 G5
Jamnagar Cl STA TW18 52 D2
Jefferson Cl DTCH/LGLY SL3 38 C1
Jellicoe Cl SL SL1 25 H4
Jennery La SL SL1 14 C3
Job's La MDHD SL6 8 B2
John Taylor Ct SL SL1 26 A3
Jordans Cl STWL/WRAY TW19 49 G1
Journeys End SLN SL2 16 C5
Jubilee Arch WDSR SL4 7 G4
Jubilee Cl STWL/WRAY TW19 49 G1
Jubilee Wy DTCH/LGLY SL3 37 G4
Juniper Dr MDHD SL6 3 J3
Jutland Pl EGH TW20 52 A1


# K


Kaywood Cl DTCH/LGLY SL3 27 G5
Keats La WDSR SL4 7 F1
Keble Rd MDHD SL6 2 B3
Keel Dr SL SL1 26 A4
Keeler Cl WDSR SL4 41 E2
Keensacre IVER SL0 19 F2
Keepers Farm Cl WDSR SL4 41 E1
Kelpatrick Rd SL SL1 24 D1
Kelsey Cl MDHD SL6 21 H5
Kempe Cl DTCH/LGLY SL3 39 E1
Kemsley Cha SLN SL2 16 A1
Kendal Cl SLN SL2 5 G1
Kendal Dr SLN SL2 27 E2
Kendrick Rd DTCH/LGLY SL3 5 K7
Kenilworth Cl SL SL1 5 F7
Kenilworth Gdns STA TW18 53 G1
Kenilworth Rd ASHF TW15 49 H4
Kenneally WDSR SL4 40 C1
Kennedy Cl MDHD SL6 21 G2
Kennet Rd MDHD SL6 3 F3
Kennett Rd DTCH/LGLY SL3 28 D5
Kent Av SLN SL2 16 A5
Kent Cl STA TW18 53 H2
Kentons La WDSR SL4 41 E1
Kent Wy MDHD SL6 12 A4
Kenwood Cl MDHD SL6 21 E1
Keppel Sp WDSR SL4 46 B1
Keppel St WDSR SL4 7 H6
Kestrel Av STA TW18 48 D4
Keswick Ct SLN SL2 5 F1
Keswick Rd EGH TW20 51 H3
Kidderminster Rd SLN SL2 15 G3
Kidwells Cl MDHD SL6 3 F3
Kidwells Park Dr MDHD SL6 3 F4
Killarney Dr MDHD SL6 2 D4
Kiln Pl MDHD SL6 11 E2
Kimber Cl WDSR SL4 41 G2
Kimberley Cl DTCH/LGLY SL3 38 B1
Kimbers Dr SL SL1 14 D3
Kimber's La MDHD SL6 22 A5
Kinburn Dr EGH TW20 51 E1
King Edward St SL SL1 4 B5
King Edward VII Av WDSR SL4 7 J2
Kingfisher Dr STA TW18 48 D5
Kinghorn La MDHD SL6 11 H2
Kinghorn Pk MDHD SL6 11 H2
King John's Cl
STWL/WRAY TW19 43 G5
Kingsbury Crs STA TW18 48 B5
Kingsbury Dr WDSR SL4 46 A1
King's Cl STA TW18 53 H3
Kingsfield WDSR SL4 34 D5
Kings Gv MDHD SL6 2 C6
Kings La EGH TW20 50 A1
MDHD SL6 8 B2
Kingsley Av EGH TW20 50 B2
King's Rd EGH TW20 47 G5
SL SL1 4 C7
WDSR SL4 7 H6
King Stable St WDSR SL4 7 G2
Kingston Crs ASHF TW15 53 G1
Kingston Rd STA TW18 49 E5
STA TW18 53 G2
King St MDHD SL6 2 E5
Kingsway STWL/WRAY TW19 49 H2
Kingswood Cl EGH TW20 46 D5
Kingswood Ct MDHD SL6 22 B4
Kingswood Creek
STWL/WRAY TW19 43 H4
Kingswood Ri EGH TW20 50 D1
Kinnaird Cl SL SL1 24 C1
Kirkwall Sp SLN SL2 16 C5
Knightsbridge Crs STA TW18 53 F2
Knights Cl EGH TW20 * 52 B2
WDSR SL4 34 D5
Knights Pl WDSR SL4 42 A2
Knolton Wy SLN SL2 27 G2
Knowle Gn STA TW18 53 E1
Knowle Park Av STA TW18 53 F2
Knowsley Cl MDHD SL6 11 E4


# L


Laburnham Rd MDHD SL6 2 B7
Laburnum Gv DTCH/LGLY SL3 38 C3
Laburnum Pl EGH TW20 50 B2
Lacey Cl EGH TW20 52 B3
Ladbrooke Rd SL SL1 26 A5
Ladyday Pl SL SL1 * 26 A3
Laggan Rd MDHD SL6 12 B3
Laggan Sq MDHD SL6 12 B4
Lake Av SL SL1 4 A1
Lake End Ct MDHD SL6 * 24 B1
Lake End Rd WDSR SL4 24 B5
Lakeside MDHD SL6 12 D3
Lakeside Dr SLN SL2 16 C1
Lakeside Rd DTCH/LGLY SL3 39 H4
Lake Vw MDHD SL6 12 C4
Laleham Cl STA TW18 53 F4
Laleham Reach CHERT KT16 53 F5
Laleham Rd STA TW18 52 D2
Lambert Av DTCH/LGLY SL3 28 A5
Lambourne Dr MDHD SL6 21 G5
Lammas Cl STA TW18 48 C4
Lammas Ct WDSR SL4 7 F7
Lammas Dr STA TW18 48 B5
Lammas Rd SL SL1 14 D5
Lancaster Av SLN SL2 16 A4
Lancaster Cl EGH TW20 50 D1
Lancaster Rd MDHD SL6 11 F5
Lancastria Ms MDHD SL6 2 B5
Lancelot Cl SL SL1 25 G4
Langdale Cl MDHD SL6 3 H5
Langham Pl EGH TW20 51 F1
Langley Broom DTCH/LGLY SL3 38 B2
Langley Pk DTCH/LGLY SL3 * 18 C5
Langley Park Rd IVER SL0 28 D2
Langley Quay
DTCH/LGLY SL3 * 28 C4
Langley Rd DTCH/LGLY SL3 27 G5
STA TW18 52 D2
Langton Cl MDHD SL6 2 A2
SL SL1 24 D3
Langton Wy EGH TW20 52 A2
Langworthy End MDHD SL6 32 D3
Langworthy La MDHD SL6 32 C3
Lansdowne Av SL SL1 4 C3
Lansdowne Ct SL SL1 4 D3
Lansdowne Rd STA TW18 53 F3
Lantern Wk MDHD SL6 3 K5
Larch Cl SLN SL2 15 H5
Larchfield Rd MDHD SL6 21 H3
Larchwood Dr EGH TW20 50 B2
Lark Av STA TW18 48 D4
Larkings La DTCH/LGLY SL3 17 F1
Larksfield EGH TW20 50 B3
La Roche Cl DTCH/LGLY SL3 27 G5
Lascelles Rd DTCH/LGLY SL3 5 K6
Lassell Gdns MDHD SL6 3 J4
Laurel Av DTCH/LGLY SL3 28 A4
EGH TW20 50 B1
Laurel Cl DTCH/LGLY SL3 39 G4
Laurels Rd IVER SL0 19 F2
Lauser Rd STWL/WRAY TW19 49 G1
Lautree Gdns MDHD SL6 9 E3
Lawkland SLN SL2 16 A3
Lawn Cl DTCH/LGLY SL3 37 G4
The Lawns DTCH/LGLY SL3 * 39 G5
The Lawn DTCH/LGLY SL3 * 37 G5
Lawrence Wy SL SL1 14 C5
Laxton Gn MDHD SL6 21 G5
Layburn Crs DTCH/LGLY SL3 38 D3
Leacroft STA TW18 53 F1
Leacroft Cl STA TW18 49 F5
Leacroft Rd IVER SL0 29 F2
Leaholme Gdns SL SL1 14 C5
Leas Dr IVER SL0 29 G1
The Leas STA TW18 * 49 E5
The Lea EGH TW20 51 H3
Ledger La MDHD SL6 33 F5
Ledger's Rd SL SL1 4 C4
Leeds Rd SL SL1 26 C2
Lee La MDHD SL6 10 C2
Lees Cl MDHD SL6 21 F3
Lees Gdns MDHD SL6 21 F3
Leeson Gdns WDSR SL4 35 E1
Leigh Pk DTCH/LGLY SL3 * 37 G4
Leigh Rd SL SL1 25 H2
Leigh Sq WDSR SL4 40 D1
Leighton Gdns MDHD SL6 3 K1
Leiston Sp SL SL1 26 C1
Leith Cl SL SL1 5 G3
Lent Green La SL SL1 14 B4
Lent Rise Rd MDHD SL6 24 B1
Lerwick Dr SLN SL2 16 C5
Lesters Rd MDHD SL6 8 D4
Lewes Ct SL SL1 26 A4
Lewins Wy SL SL1 25 F2
Lexington Av MDHD SL6 21 G3
Leylands La STWL/WRAY TW19 45 H4
Liddell WDSR SL4 40 C2
Lightlands La MDHD SL6 9 F5
Lilley Wy SL SL1 25 E3
Lillibrooke Crs MDHD SL6 21 E5
Lime Av WDSR SL4 36 D4
Limes Rd EGH TW20 51 F1
The Limes WDSR SL4 40 C1
Lime Wk MDHD SL6 11 E4
Linchfield Rd DTCH/LGLY SL3 37 G5
Lincoln Hatch La SL SL1 14 C4
Lincoln Rd MDHD SL6 11 F5
Lincoln Wy SL SL1 24 D2
Linden Av MDHD SL6 2 A1
Linden Ct EGH TW20 50 B2
Linden Dr SLN SL2 16 A1
Lindores Rd MDHD SL6 32 D3
Lingholm Cl MDHD SL6 21 G2
Link Rd DTCH/LGLY SL3 37 G4
Linkswood Rd SL SL1 14 C2
The Link SLN SL2 27 F1
Link Wy STA TW18 53 F2
Lismore Pk SLN SL2 26 D1
Litcham Sp SL SL1 26 B1
Littlebrook Av SL SL1 15 E5
Little Buntings WDSR SL4 41 F2
Littlecroft Rd EGH TW20 51 F1
Littledown Rd SL SL1 4 E2
Littlefield Gn MDHD SL6 30 D5
Littleport Sp SL SL1 26 C1
Little Sutton La
DTCH/LGLY SL3 38 D3
Little Woodlands WDSR SL4 41 F2
Liverpool Rd SL SL1 25 H1
Lochinvar Cl SL SL1 25 H4
Lock Av MDHD SL6 13 E3
Lockbridge Ct MDHD SL6 13 E5
Locke Gdns SLN SL2 27 G4
Lockets Cl WDSR SL4 34 D5
Lock La MDHD SL6 21 G4
Lock Md MDHD SL6 13 E3
Lock Pth WDSR SL4 34 D3
Loddon Dr MDHD SL6 2 A2
Loddon Sp SL SL1 26 C2
Lodge Cl EGH TW20 50 D1
SL SL1 26 A4
Lodge Wy WDSR SL4 41 E2
London Rd DTCH/LGLY SL3 27 G5
DTCH/LGLY SL3 37 G4
EGH TW20 50 C3
STA TW18 48 D5
STWL/WRAY TW19 49 H3
Longbourn WDSR SL4 41 G2
Long Dr SL SL1 14 C3
Long Furlong Dr SLN SL2 15 E4
Long La MDHD SL6 8 C5
Longleat Gdns MDHD SL6 2 A7
Longmead WDSR SL4 35 E5
Long Readings La SLN SL2 15 H3
Longside Cl EGH TW20 52 A4
Longstone Rd IVER SL0 19 E2
Long Wk WDSR SL4 * 42 B4
The Long Wk WDSR SL4 7 J7

Longworth Dr MDHD SL6 .....13 E4
Lonsdale CI MDHD SL6 .....12 C4
Lonsdale Wy MDHD SL6 .....33 E2
Loosen Dr MDHD SL6 .....21 E5
Loring Rd WDSR SL4 .....35 F5
Lorne CI SL SL1 .....25 H5
Losfield Rd WDSR SL4 .....35 F5
Lossie Dr IVER SLO .....28 D2
Love Green La IVER SLO .....2 B6
Love Hill La DTCH/LGLY SL3 .....28 C5
Lovejoy La WDSR SL4 .....40 D1
Love La IVER SLO .....29 F1
Lovett Gdns MDHD SL6 .....13 E2
Lovett Rd EGH TW20 .....47 H5
Lowbrook Dr MDHD SL6 .....21 E5
Lower Boyndon Rd MDHD SL6 .....2 B2
Lower Britwell Rd SL SL1 .....14 D4
Lower Cippenham La SL SL1 .....25 F3
Lower Cookham Rd MDHD SL6 .....12 B2
Lower Lees Rd SLN SL2 .....15 G3
Lower Md IVER SLO .....19 F3
Lower Rd WDSR SL4 .....9 F3
Lowestoft Dr SL SL1 .....24 C1
Lucan Dr STA TW18 .....53 H3
Luddington Av EGH TW20 .....51 F5
Ludlow Rd MDHD SL6 .....22 A3
Luff CI WDSR SL4 .....41 E2
Lydford Av SLN SL2 .....16 B5
Lydsey CI SLN SL2 .....15 G3
Lyell Rd WDSR SL4 .....40 D1
Lynch Hill La SL SL1 .....15 E4
Lynden CI MDHD SL6 .....32 D3
Lyndhurst Av MDHD SL6 *.....6 A2
Lyndwood Dr WDSR SL4 .....43 E5
Lyndwood Pde WDSR SL4 *.....43 E5
Lyneham Gdns MDHD SL6 .....11 F4
Lynton Gn MDHD SL6 .....2 C4
Lynwood Av DTCH/LGLY SL3 .....27 H5
    EGH TW20 .....51 E2

**M**

Mackenzie St SL SL1 .....4 E4
Madeira Wk WDSR SL4 .....47 H5
Mafeking Rd
    STWL/WRAY TW19 .....47 H3
Magna Carta La
    STWL/WRAY TW19 .....46 D2
Magna Rd EGH TW20 .....50 B2
Magnolia Gdns DTCH/LGLY SL3 .....5 K6
Maidenhead Court Pk
    MDHD SL6 .....12 D2
Maidenhead Rd MDHD SL6 .....12 A1
    WDSR SL4 .....8 B4
Maiden Hythe PI MDHD SL6 .....2 B4
Main Dr IVER SLO .....29 C5
Maidn Rd WDSR SL4 *.....34 C4
Maise Webster CI
    STWL/WRAY TW19 *.....49 H1
Major's Farm Rd
    DTCH/LGLY SL3 .....37 H4
Malders La MDHD SL6 .....11 F2
Malet CI EGH TW20 *.....52 B2
Mallard Dr SL SL1 .....5 J1
The Mallards STA TW18 .....53 F5
Mallow Pk MDHD SL6 .....11 G4
Malpas Rd SLN SL2 .....5 J1
Malt HI EGH TW20 .....51 E1
Malt House CI WDSR SL4 .....46 B1
The Maltings STA TW18 .....48 C5
Malton Av SL SL1 .....4 A1
Malvern Rd MDHD SL6 .....11 H4
Manfield CI SL SL1 .....25 F3
Manor Ct SL SL1 .....25 H5
Manorcrofts Rd EGH TW20 .....51 G2
Manor Farm Av WDSR SL4 *.....41 F2
Manor Farm Cottages
    WDSR SL4 .....43 E4
Manor Farm Ct SL SL1 .....51 G1
Manor Farm La SL SL1 .....51 G1
Manor Gv MDHD SL6 .....33 F5
Manor House La
    DTCH/LGLY SL3 .....37 F5
Manor La MDHD SL6 .....22 A4
Manor Leaze EGH TW20 .....51 H1
Manor Pk STA TW18 .....48 B4
Manor PI STA TW18 .....53 F1
Manor Rd MDHD SL6 .....22 A3
    WDSR SL4 .....41 E1
Manor Wy EGH TW20 .....51 F2
    MDHD SL6 .....32 C3
Mansel CI SLN SL2 .....17 F5
Mansel CI WDSR SL4 .....41 E1
Mansion La IVER SLO .....29 E3
Maple CI MDHD SL6 .....21 F5
Maple Ct EGH TW20 .....50 B2
Maple Crs SLN SL2 .....5 K1
Maplin Pk DTCH/LGLY SL3 .....28 D5
Marbeck CI WDSR SL4 .....34 D5
Marcia Ct SL SL1 .....25 F3
Marescroft Rd SLN SL2 .....15 F4
Margaret Ct STA TW18 .....53 H5
Marina Pde STA TW18 * .....53 F4
Marina Wy IVER SLO .....29 H2
    SL SL1 .....24 D2
Marish Whf DTCH/LGLY SL3 *.....28 A4
Market La DTCH/LGLY SL3 .....39 G5
Market PI DTCH/LGLY SL3 .....39 E4
Market St MDHD SL6 .....2 E5
    WDSR SL4 .....7 H4
Marlborough Rd
    DTCH/LGLY SL3 .....37 H1
Marlow Rd MDHD SL6 .....2 D4
    MDHD SL6 .....10 C1
Marshfield DTCH/LGLY SL3 .....37 G5
Marsh La MDHD SL6 .....23 H4
Martin CI WDSR SL4 .....34 C5
Martindale IVER SLO .....19 E4
Martin Rd MDHD SL6 .....2 A6
    SL SL1 .....4 C6
Martin's Pln SLN SL2 .....16 D3

Marunden Gn SLN SL2 .....15 F3
Maryside DTCH/LGLY SL3 .....28 A4
Masons Rd SL SL1 .....25 E2
Mathisen Wy DTCH/LGLY SL3 .....39 G5
Matthew Arnold CI STA TW18 .....53 G2
Matthews La STA TW18 .....48 D5
Maybury Ct SL SL1 .....14 D5
Mayfield Dr WDSR SL4 .....41 G2
Mayfield Gdns STA TW18 .....52 D3
Maypole Rd MDHD SL6 .....14 A5
Mead Av DTCH/LGLY SL3 .....28 D4
Mead CI DTCH/LGLY SL3 .....28 D4
    EGH TW20 .....51 H2
Mead Ct EGH TW20 .....52 A2
Meadfield Av DTCH/LGLY SL3 .....28 C5
Meadfield Rd DTCH/LGLY SL3 .....28 D5
Meadowbrook CI
    DTCH/LGLY SL3 .....45 G1
Meadow Ct WDSR SL4 .....43 F5
Meadow Ct STA TW18 .....48 C4
Meadow La WDSR SL4 .....6 E2
Meadow Rd DTCH/LGLY SL3 .....28 A5
Meadow Vw
    STWL/WRAY TW19 .....45 H4
Meadow View La MDHD SL6 .....32 A3
Meadow Wy MDHD SL6 .....23 H4
    MDHD SL6 .....33 F5
    WDSR SL4 .....43 F5
Mead Wy DTCH/LGLY SL3 .....28 D4
Mead Wy SL SL1 .....14 D5
Meadway STA TW18 .....53 E5
Meadway DTCH/LGLY SL3 .....52 D3
Medallion PI MDHD SL6 .....3 K5
Mede CI STWL/WRAY TW19 .....46 D2
Medhurst Rd EGH TW20 .....52 A2
Melbourne Av SL SL1 .....26 A1
Melton Ct MDHD SL6 .....15 H4
Mendip CI DTCH/LGLY SL3 .....38 C2
Mercian Wy SL SL1 .....25 E3
Mercia Rd MDHD SL6 .....21 F4
Mere Rd SL SL1 .....5 F6
Merlin CI DTCH/LGLY SL3 *.....38 D3
Merton CI MDHD SL6 .....21 G1
    SL SL1 .....5 G6
Merwin Wy WDSR SL4 *.....40 D2
Michael CI MDHD SL6 .....21 G3
Midcroft SLN SL2 .....15 H4
Middle Gn DTCH/LGLY SL3 .....28 A2
Middlegreen Rd
    DTCH/LGLY SL3 .....27 H4
Middle HI EGH TW20 .....50 C1
Middle Wk SL SL1 .....14 B3
Midway CI STA TW18 .....49 F4
Mildenhall Rd SL SL1 .....26 C2
Milford Ct SL SL1 * .....5 H5
Millbrook Wy DTCH/LGLY SL3 .....45 G1
Millers CI STA TW18 .....53 F1
Mill La DTCH/LGLY SL3 .....44 D2
    MDHD SL6 .....9 H3
    SLN SL2 .....13 G5
    WDSR SL4 .....6 B5
Mill Md STA TW18 .....48 D5
Mill PI DTCH/LGLY SL3 .....43 H1
Millside Pk WDSR SL4 .....40 D1
Mills Sp WDSR SL4 .....46 B1
Millstream La SL SL1 .....25 E5
Mill St DTCH/LGLY SL3 .....39 F4
    SL SL1 .....5 H5
Milner Rd SL SL1 .....14 A5
Milton CI DTCH/LGLY SL3 .....44 C2
Milton Pk EGH TW20 .....51 G3
Milton Rd EGH TW20 .....51 F1
    SL SL1 .....5 F1
Milverton CI MDHD SL6 .....21 F5
Mina Av DTCH/LGLY SL3 .....27 H4
Minniecroft Rd SL SL1 .....14 B3
Minster Wy DTCH/LGLY SL3 .....28 B4
Minton Ri MDHD SL6 .....9 H6
Mirador Crs SLN SL2 .....27 F2
Missenden Gdns SL SL1 .....24 B1
Mitchell CI SL SL1 .....25 C5
Moat Dr SL SL1 .....17 G5
Moffy HI MDHD SL6 .....12 A3
Molyns Ms SL SL1 .....25 E3
Monastery Gdns
    DTCH/LGLY SL3 *.....43 F2
Moneyrow Gn MDHD SL6 .....32 C4
Monkey Island La MDHD SL6 .....33 F5
Monksfield Wy SLN SL2 .....15 G4
Monks Rd WDSR SL4 .....40 D1
Monks Wy DTCH/LGLY SL3 .....44 C2
Mons Wk STA TW18 .....52 A1
Montague Rd SL SL1 .....26 D2
Montagu Rd DTCH/LGLY SL3 .....37 F5
Montem La SL SL1 .....4 A4
Montgomery Rd SL SL1 .....27 G1
Montpellier Ct WDSR SL4 .....7 F7
Montrose Av DTCH/LGLY SL3 .....37 G4
    SL SL1 .....25 H1
Montrose Dr MDHD SL6 .....21 E2
Montrose Wy DTCH/LGLY SL3 .....37 H5
Monycrower Dr MDHD SL6 .....2 C5
Moorbridge Rd MDHD SL6 .....2 E3
Moore CI SL SL1 .....25 H4
Moore Grove Crs EGH TW20 .....51 E5
Moor End MDHD SL6 .....33 E2
Moores La SL SL1 .....35 F1
Moorfields CI STA TW18 .....52 C4
Moorfield Ter MDHD SL6 .....3 H3
Moor Furlong SL SL1 .....24 B1
The Moorings
    STWL/WRAY TW19 .....46 C1
    MDHD SL6 .....34 D4
Moorlands Dr MDHD SL6 .....10 D5
Moor La MDHD SL6 .....12 B4
    SLN SL2 .....13 G4
    STA TW18 .....48 A2
    STWL/WRAY TW19 .....46 D2
Moormede Crs STA TW18 .....48 D5
Moorside CI MDHD SL6 .....12 B4
Moorstown Ct SL SL1 .....4 D5
Moor Dr SLN SL2 .....27 E1
Moreau Wk DTCH/LGLY SL3 .....28 A1
Moreland CI DTCH/LGLY SL3 .....39 E4
Morello Dr DTCH/LGLY SL3 .....28 B3

Moretaine Rd ASHF TW15 .....49 H4
Moreton Wy SL SL1 .....24 D3
Morley CI DTCH/LGLY SL3 .....28 B4
Morrice CI DTCH/LGLY SL3 .....38 B1
Mortimer Rd DTCH/LGLY SL3 .....27 H5
Mossy V MDHD SL6 .....11 H4
Mountbatten Ct SL SL1 .....5 G7
Mountbatten Sq WDSR SL4 .....7 G6
Mount Lee EGH TW20 .....51 E1
Mowbray Crs EGH TW20 .....51 G1
Mulberry Av WDSR SL4 .....42 D2
Mulberry Dr DTCH/LGLY SL3 .....38 A2
Mulberry Wk MDHD SL6 *.....7 F5
Mullens Rd EGH TW20 .....51 J4
Mundesley Sp SL SL1 .....26 C1
Murdoch CI STA TW18 .....53 E1
Murrin Rd MDHD SL6 .....21 G1
Mustard Mill Rd STA TW18 .....48 D5
The Myrke DTCH/LGLY SL3 .....36 D1
Myrtle CI DTCH/LGLY SL3 .....39 G5
Myrtle Crs SLN SL2 .....26 D2

**N**

Napier Rd MDHD SL6 .....21 F2
Nash Rd DTCH/LGLY SL3 .....38 B2
Needham CI MDHD SL6 .....35 E5
Nelson CI DTCH/LGLY SL3 .....37 H1
Nelson Rd WDSR SL4 .....41 F2
Newberry Crs WDSR SL4 .....34 C5
Newbery Wy SL SL1 .....4 B5
Newbury Dr MDHD SL6 .....3 J6
Newchurch Rd SLN SL2 .....15 H4
Newhaven Sp SLN SL2 * .....15 H4
Newlands Dr DTCH/LGLY SL3 .....45 G2
    MDHD SL6 .....21 E1
Newport Rd SL SL1 .....14 D5
New Rd DTCH/LGLY SL3 .....28 C5
    DTCH/LGLY SL3 .....37 H5
    MDHD SL6 .....3 D3
    MDHD SL6 .....33 D5
    STA TW18 .....52 A1
New Sq SL SL1 .....4 E4
New St SL SL1 * .....49 E5
Newton CI DTCH/LGLY SL3 .....28 B4
Newton Rd WDSR SL4 .....43 E5
Newton La WDSR SL4 .....43 E5
Newtonside Orch WDSR SL4 *.....43 E5
New Wickham La EGH TW20 .....51 G5
Nicholas Gdns SL SL1 .....25 E3
Nicholls WDSR SL4 .....40 C2
Nicholson Ms EGH TW20 *.....51 G1
Nicholsons La MDHD SL6 .....2 E4
Nicholsons Wk MDHD SL6 .....3 F5
Nicholson Wk EGH TW20 .....51 G1
Nightingale Ct SL SL1 .....5 G6
Nightingale La MDHD SL6 .....11 H2
Nightingale PI MDHD SL6 * .....9 F4
Nightingale Shott EGH TW20 .....51 F2
Nightingale Wk WDSR SL4 .....42 A2
Nine Acres SL SL1 .....25 F3
Nixey CI SL SL1 .....5 H5
Nobles Wy EGH TW20 .....50 C3
Norden CI MDHD SL6 .....21 G4
Norden Mdw MDHD SL6 .....21 G3
Norden Rd MDHD SL6 .....21 G4
Norelands Dr SL SL1 .....14 C2
Norfolk Av SL SL1 .....16 A5
Norfolk Park Cottages
    MDHD SL6 .....2 E2
Norfolk Rd MDHD SL6 .....2 A6
Norlands La EGH TW20 .....52 C5
Normandy Wk EGH TW20 *.....52 A1
The Normans SLN SL2 .....27 F1
Norreys Dr MDHD SL6 .....21 H4
Northampton Av SL SL1 .....26 A1
Northborough Rd SLN SL2 .....15 H4
North Burnham CI SLN SL2 .....14 B2
North CI WDSR SL4 .....35 F5
Northcroft SL SL1 .....26 A2
Northcroft Gdns EGH TW20 .....50 B1
Northcroft Rd EGH TW20 .....50 B1
Northcroft Vs EGH TW20 .....50 B1
North Dean MDHD SL6 .....2 A1
Northern Rd SLN SL2 .....16 B4
Northfield Ct STA TW18 .....53 F4
Northfield Rd MDHD SL6 .....12 B4
    STA TW18 .....53 F4
    WDSR SL4 .....35 F1
North Gn MDHD SL6 .....3 F1
    SL SL1 .....5 F1
Northmead Rd SLN SL2 .....15 F4
North Pk IVER SLO .....29 G5
North Rd MDHD SL6 .....12 D5
North Star La MDHD SL6 .....2 D5
North St EGH TW20 .....51 F1
North Town CI MDHD SL6 .....3 F1
North Town Md MDHD SL6 .....12 D4
North Town Moor MDHD SL6 .....12 D4
North Town Rd MDHD SL6 .....12 B4
Northumbria Rd MDHD SL6 .....11 F4
Norway Dr SLN SL2 .....17 F5
Norwood La IVER SLO .....19 G5
Notley End EGH TW20 .....50 C3
Nursery Gdns STA TW18 .....53 F5
Nursery La DTCH/LGLY SL3 .....27 G3
Nursery PI WDSR SL4 .....43 G5
Nursery Rd MDHD SL6 .....24 B1
Nursery Wy STWL/WRAY TW19 .....43 H5

**O**

Oak Av EGH TW20 .....52 A3
Oak End Dr IVER SLO .....19 E2
Oaken Gv MDHD SL6 .....11 G4
Oakfield Av SL SL1 .....25 H3
Oakhurst MDHD SL6 .....12 D1
Oak La EGH TW20 .....46 C4

Oakley Crs SL SL1 .....26 C2
Oakley Green Rd WDSR SL4 .....34 B5
The Oaks STA TW18 * .....48 D5
Oak Stubbs La MDHD SL6 .....23 H4
Oak Tree Dr EGH TW20 .....50 C1
Oast House CI
    STWL/WRAY TW19 .....47 E1
Oatlands Dr SL SL1 .....4 B3
Oban Ct SL SL1 .....4 B4
The Observatory SL SL1 * .....5 H5
Ockwells Rd MDHD SL6 .....21 F5
Octavia Wy STA TW18 .....53 E2
Odencroft Rd SLN SL2 .....15 G3
Odney La MDHD SL6 .....12 C1
Oldacres MDHD SL6 .....3 K5
Old Court CI MDHD SL6 .....21 F5
Old Crown SL SL1 * .....4 E4
Oldershaw Ms MDHD SL6 .....9 H6
Old Ferry Dr STWL/WRAY TW19 .....43 C5
Oldfield Rd MDHD SL6 .....3 J6
Oldfield Vw MDHD SL6 * .....23 E4
Old Fives Ct SL SL1 .....14 C3
Old Forge CI MDHD SL6 * .....22 C5
Old Mill La DTCH/LGLY SL3 *.....27 H1
Old Marsh La MDHD SL6 .....33 G4
Old Mill La MDHD SL6 .....23 F5
Old Mill PI STWL/WRAY TW19 .....44 D5
Old Post Office La MDHD SL6 .....9 F4
Old School Ct
    STWL/WRAY TW19 .....47 E1
Old Slade La DTCH/LGLY SL3 .....39 H2
Old Station La
    STWL/WRAY TW19 .....44 B5
Oldway La SL SL1 .....24 D3
Omega Wy EGH TW20 .....52 A4
Opal Ct DTCH/LGLY SL3 .....17 G4
Opendale Rd SL SL1 .....14 D5
Orchard Av SL SL1 .....14 D5
    WDSR SL4 .....42 A4
Orchard CI MDHD SL6 .....22 C5
Orchard Gv MDHD SL6 .....21 G1
Orchard MI BNEND SL8 .....9 H1
Orchard Rd MDHD SL6 .....46 B1
Orchardville SL SL1 .....14 B4
Orchard Wy DTCH/LGLY SL3 .....28 A3
Orchid Ct EGH TW20 .....47 H5
Orwell CI WDSR SL4 .....42 B2
Osborne CI MDHD SL6 .....12 D4
Osborne Ms WDSR SL4 .....7 F7
Osborne Rd EGH TW20 .....51 F2
    SL SL1 .....5 F5
Osborne St SL SL1 .....5 F5
Osier PI EGH TW20 .....52 A2
Osney Rd MDHD SL6 .....12 A3
Ostler Ga MDHD SL6 .....21 E5
Ouseley Rd STWL/WRAY TW19 .....46 C1
Oxford Av SL SL1 .....14 A2
    WDSR SL4 .....7 H5
Oxford Rd WDSR SL4 .....6 D4
Oxford Rd East WDSR SL4 .....7 F5

**P**

The Paddock DTCH/LGLY SL3 .....37 F5
    MDHD SL6 .....12 D1
    WDSR SL4 * .....34 C4
Padstow CI DTCH/LGLY SL3 .....28 A5
Pages Whf DTCH/LGLY SL6 * .....23 E1
Paget Dr MDHD SL6 .....21 E4
Paget Rd DTCH/LGLY SL3 .....38 B1
The Pagoda MDHD SL6 .....12 D4
Palace CI SL SL1 .....25 F3
Paley St MDHD SL6 .....31 F5
Palmers CI MDHD SL6 .....21 E5
Palmerston Av DTCH/LGLY SL3 .....5 K6
Pamela Rw MDHD SL6 * .....32 C5
Pantile Rw DTCH/LGLY SL3 .....38 C1
The Parade STA TW18 * .....38 C1
    STA TW18 .....52 A3
    STWL/WRAY TW19 .....43 H4
Park CI WDSR SL4 .....7 H6
Park Cnr MDHD SL6 .....10 D2
Park La DTCH/LGLY SL3 .....37 H2
Parkland Av DTCH/LGLY SL3 .....37 H2
Park La DTCH/LGLY SL3 .....5 K7
    SLN SL2 .....16 B2
Parkside MDHD SL6 .....2 B1
Parkside PI STA TW18 .....53 E2
Parkside Wk DTCH/LGLY SL3 .....39 F5
    MDHD SL6 .....10 D1
    SL SL1 .....16 B2
    WDSR SL4 .....7 H5
Park Vw MDHD SL6 .....2 E4
Parkview Cha SL SL1 .....25 E1
The Parkway IVER SLO .....19 E1
Parr Gn North DTCH/LGLY SL3 .....38 D1
    IVER SLO .....18 D2
Parry Gn South
    DTCH/LGLY SL3 .....38 C1
Parsonage La WDSR SL4 .....6 B5
Parsonage Rd EGH TW20 .....50 D1
Parsons Rd DTCH/LGLY SL3 .....37 F5
Partridge Md MDHD SL6 .....32 B5
Patricia CI SL SL1 .....25 E2
Pavilion Gdns STA TW18 .....53 F5
Paxton Av SL SL1 .....26 A5
Peace La MDHD SL6 .....9 E4
Peace Rd DTCH/LGLY SL3 .....18 C5
    MDHD SL6 .....9 E4
Pearce Dr MDHD SL6 .....12 B4
Pearce Rd MDHD SL6 .....12 B4
Pearl Gdns SL SL1 .....25 H3
Peartree CI SL SL1 .....25 H3
Peascod St WDSR SL4 .....7 F5
Peel CI WDSR SL4 .....41 H2

Peel Ct SL SL1 .....
Peket CI STA TW18 .....
Peiling HI WDSR SL4 .....
Pemberton Rd SLN SL2 .....
Penling CI MDHD SL6 .....
Pennine Rd SLN SL2 .....
Penn Meadow SLN SL2 .....
    SLN SL2 .....
Penrose Ct EGH TW20 .....
Penshurst Rd MDHD SL6 .....
Pentland Rd SLN SL2 .....
Penton Av STA TW18 .....
Penton Hall Dr STA TW18 .....
Penton Hook Rd STA TW18 .....
Penton Rd STA TW18 .....
Penwood Ct MDHD SL6 .....
Penyston Rd MDHD SL6 .....
Penzance Sp SLN SL2 .....
Pepler Wy SL SL1 .....
Pepys CI DTCH/LGLY SL3 .....
Perrycroft WDSR SL4 .....
Perryfields Wy SL SL1 .....
Perryman Wy SLN SL2 .....
Perth Av SL SL1 .....
Peterhead Ms DTCH/LGLY SL3 .....
Petersfield Av SLN SL2 .....
    STA TW18 .....
Petersfield Rd STA TW18 .....
Peters La MDHD SL6 .....
Petty Cross SL SL1 .....
Pevensey Rd SL SL1 .....
Pheasants Cft MDHD SL6 .....
Philbye Ms SL SL1 .....
Philip Rd STA TW18 .....
Phipps CI MDHD SL6 .....
Phipps Rd SL SL1 .....
Pickford Dr DTCH/LGLY SL3 .....
Pickfords Gdns SL SL1 .....
Pickins Piece DTCH/LGLY SL3 .....
Pierson Rd WDSR SL4 .....
Pine CI MDHD SL6 .....
Pine Trees STA TW18 * .....
Pinewood Dr STA TW18 * .....
Pinewood Rd IVER SLO .....
Pink La SL SL1 .....
Pinkneys Dr MDHD SL6 .....
Pinkneys Rd MDHD SL6 .....
Pipers CI SL SL1 .....
The Pippins DTCH/LGLY SL3 .....
Pitts Rd SL SL1 .....
Plackett Wy SL SL1 .....
Plaines CI SL SL1 .....
Plough La SL SL1 .....
Ploughlees La SL SL1 .....
Plover CI STA TW18 .....
Plymouth Rd SL SL1 .....
Pococks La WDSR SL4 .....
The Points MDHD SL6 .....
Pollard CI WDSR SL4 .....
Pond Rd EGH TW20 .....
Pooley Av EGH TW20 .....
Pooley Green Rd EGH TW20 .....
Pool La SL SL1 .....
Poolmans Rd WDSR SL4 .....
Popes CI DTCH/LGLY SL3 .....
Popes La MDHD SL6 .....
Poplar CI DTCH/LGLY SL3 .....
Poplars Gv MDHD SL6 .....
Portland CI SL SL1 .....
Portlock Rd MDHD SL6 .....
Post Meadow IVER SLO .....
Post Office La DTCH/LGLY SL3 .....
Potters Cross IVER SLO .....
Poulcott STWL/WRAY TW19 .....
Poundfield La MDHD SL6 .....
The Pound MDHD SL6 .....
Powis CI MDHD SL6 .....
Powney Rd MDHD SL6 .....
Poyle La SL SL1 .....
Poyle Rd DTCH/LGLY SL3 * .....
Poyle Rd DTCH/LGLY SL3 .....
The Poynings IVER SLO .....
The Precincts SL SL1 .....
The Precinct EGH TW20 * .....
Prescott Rd DTCH/LGLY SL3 .....
Preston Rd SLN SL2 .....
Prestwood SL SL1 .....
Priest HI EGH TW20 .....
Primrose La MDHD SL6 .....
Prince Andrew CI MDHD SL6 .....
Prince Andrew Rd MDHD SL6 .....
Prince Consort Cottages
    WDSR SL4 .....
Prince Consort's Dr WDSR SL4 .....41
Princes CI WDSR SL4 .....35
Princes Rd EGH TW20 .....
Princess Av WDSR SL4 .....41
Princes St SL SL1 .....5
Priors CI MDHD SL6 .....
    SL SL1 .....
Priors Rd WDSR SL4 .....40
Priory Ct STA TW18 .....
Priory Gn STA TW18 .....
Priory Ms STA TW18 .....
Priory Rd SL SL1 .....
Priory Wy DTCH/LGLY SL3 .....57
Prospect La EGH TW20 .....
Prospect PI STA TW18 .....
Providence PI MDHD SL6 .....
Prune HI EGH TW20 .....50
Pudseys CI MDHD SL6 .....8
Pullmans PI STA TW18 .....
Pursers CI SL SL1 .....21
Pursell CI MDHD SL6 .....

**Q**

Quantock CI DTCH/LGLY SL3 .....38
Quaves Rd DTCH/LGLY SL3 .....5

Anne's Rd WDSR SL4 ....42 A3
Elizabeth's Wk
  SR SL4 ....7 K6
s Acre WDSR SL4 ....42 B3
's Cl WDSR SL4 ....43 E4
s Ct SL SL1 * ....5 F1
's Dr DTCH/LGLY SL3 ....18 B1
s La MDHD SL6 ....5 F2
nsmead DTCH/LGLY SL3 ....37 F5
nsmere Rd SL SL1 ....5 J5
nsmere Rd SL SL1 ....5 J5
n's Rd DTCH/LGLY SL3 ....37 F5
  TW20 ....51 J2
  SL1 ....6 E7
s St MDHD SL6 ....3 F6
ns Wk ASHF TW15 ....49 H5
nsway MDHD SL6 ....12 A3
Victoria's Wk WDSR SL4 ....7 K4
rookes SLN SL2 ....5 G7
y Rd EGH TW20 ....51 G1

## R

ot Av DTCH/LGLY SL3 ....28 D5
ot Cl MDHD SL6 ....12 A2
or Wy DTCH/LGLY SL3 ....38 A1
tone Rd SL SL1 ....4 C6
ray Ter SLN SL2 ....4 E2
s Ct SL SL1 * ....52 B1
aw TW18
ray Vw DTCH/LGLY SL3 * ....44 B2
sborough Cha MDHD SL6 ....11 H5
gh Cl SL1 ....25 G3
gh Ct STA TW18 ....53 F5
oler Cl MDHD SL6 ....24 B1
oler La DTCH/LGLY SL3 ....27 G5
sey Ct SL SL1 ....14 D4
all Cl DTCH/LGLY SL3 ....38 B2
olph Rd DTCH/LGLY SL3 ....38 A1
nsdale Ms STA TW18 ....53 F2
ners Fld DTCH/LGLY SL3 ....27 H4
nsfield EGH TW20 ....50 B2
nsworth Rd SLN SL2 ....15 C3
ot MDHD SL6 ....3 K4
Lea MDHD SL6 ....3 J2
Lea Rd MDHD SL6 ....3 J2
Lodge Ms MDHD SL6 ....3 J3
Mead Ct MDHD SL6 ....13 E4
Meadow Rd MDHD SL6 ....3 K4
Mead Rd MDHD SL6 ....13 E5
Mill Rd East MDHD SL6 ....13 F5
Mill Rd West MDHD SL6 ....13 E5
mond Cl DTCH/LGLY SL3 ....39 G5
mond Rd DTCH/LGLY SL3 ....38 C1
ers Cl DTCH/LGLY SL3 ....39 E4
Park Av MDHD SL6 ....13 F5
Park La MDHD SL6 ....3 J3
Park Rd MDHD SL6 ....13 E5
s Av WDSR SL4 ....35 F4
St MDHD SL6 ....13 E5
cory Cl SLN SL2 ....16 A3
cory Rd MDHD SL6 ....13 F4
Cottage Ms
  TCH/LGLY SL3 ....27 G5
ct SL SL1 * ....11 J2
dington Dr DTCH/LGLY SL3 ....38 B1
ford Rd WDSR SL4 ....34 D5
riff Cl MDHD SL6 ....2 B7
wood EGH TW20 ....50 C2
  SL SL1 ....14 A2
wood Gdns SL SL1 ....5 G7
Redwoods WDSR SL4 ....42 B2
d Cl IVER SLO ....29 G1
re Rd MDHD SL6 ....32 D3
orn Rd MDHD SL6 ....3 J5
nie Cl MDHD SL6 ....32 D1
ent Ct MDHD SL6 * ....2 E5
Ave MDHD SL6 ....3 J4
nie Cl ASHF TW15 ....49 H4
ton Cl MDHD SL6 ....21 G5
Retreat EGH TW20 ....50 D2
  MDHD SL6 ....33 F4
esby Cl MDHD SL6 ....21 H5
odes Ct EGH TW20 * ....52 A1
ardo Rd MDHD SL6 ....21 F5
nards Wy SL SL1 ....25 G3
hings Wy IVER SLO ....29 H5
mond Crs SL SL1 * ....52 D1
  TW18 * ....52 D1
mond Rd STA TW18 ....52 D1
gebank SL SL1 ....25 F2
gemead Rd EGH TW20 ....66 B4
ge Wy IVER SLO ....29 G2
ing Court Rd
  OTCH/LGLY SL3 ....37 G5
e Ridings IVER SLO ....39 H1
  MDHD SL6 ....20 D1
  WDSR SL4 ....34 C4
ey Av EGH TW20 ....51 E2
ey Cl DTCH/LGLY SL3 ....38 A1
borough Rd MDHD SL6 ....2 D2
e Hag HI MDHD SL6 ....24 A1
eley Rd MDHD SL6 ....4 A5
a Riverbank WDSR SL4 ....23 E1
er Ct MDHD SL6 ....23 E1
erfield Rd STA TW18 ....52 D2
er Gdns MDHD SL6 ....21 F5
er Park Av TW18 ....48 B5
er Rd MDHD SL6 ....23 E1
  STA TW18 ....52 D4
  WDSR SL4 ....34 C4
erside BNEND SL8 ....9 H1
erside CHERT KT16 * ....54 B1
  MDHD SL6 ....46 C1
  STWL/WRAY TW19 ....
erside Ct STA TW18 ....52 D4
erside Dr STA TW18 ....52 D1
erside Rd STA TW18 ....52 D3

Riverside Wk WDSR SL4 ....7 H3
River St WDSR SL4 ....7 G3
Riverway STA TW18 ....53 F4
Riverwood Av MLW SL7 ....8 A1
Riverwoods Dr MLW SL7 ....8 A1
Rixman Cl MDHD SL6 ....21 H5
Rixon Ct DTCH/LGLY SL3 ....28 A1
Roberts Wy EGH TW20 ....50 C3
Robin Hood Cl SL SL1 ....25 E5
Robin Wy STA TW18 ....48 D4
Robin Willis Wy WDSR SL4 ....43 E5
Rochester Rd EGH TW20 ....52 B1
Rochfords Gdns SLN SL2 ....27 G3
Rochford Wy MDHD SL6 ....24 A2
Rockall Ct DTCH/LGLY SL3 ....28 D5
Rodney Wy DTCH/LGLY SL3 ....39 G5
Roebuck Gn SL SL1 ....25 E5
Rogers La SLN SL2 ....16 D1
Rokesby Rd SL SL1 ....15 F3
Rolls La MDHD SL6 ....32 A3
Romana Ct STA TW18 * ....49 E5
Roman Lea MDHD SL6 ....9 F5
Romney Lock Rd WDSR SL4 ....7 H2
Romsey Ct DTCH/LGLY SL3 ....28 B5
Ronaldsay Sp SLN SL2 ....16 C5
Rookery Rd STA TW18 ....53 F1
Rosebank Cl MDHD SL6 ....9 E5
Rosefield Rd STA TW18 ....49 E5
Rose Gdns STWL/WRAY TW19 ....49 F2
Rose HI SL SL1 ....14 A1
Roseleigh Cl MDHD SL6 ....21 E1
Roses La WDSR SL4 ....40 D1
Rosken Cl SL SL1 ....15 H5
Rosken Gv SLN SL2 ....15 H2
Rossiter Cl DTCH/LGLY SL3 ....38 A1
Ross Rd MDHD SL6 ....21 H5
Rostrevor Gdns IVER SLO ....44 D1
Roundway EGH TW20 ....52 A1
Rowan Av EGH TW20 ....52 A1
Rowan Gdns IVER SLO ....19 E2
Rowan Wy SL SL1 ....15 H5
Rowland Ct WDSR SL4 ....40 D2
Rowley La DTCH/LGLY SL3 ....18 A2
Roxwell Cl SL SL1 ....25 E3
Royston Wy SL SL1 ....14 D5
Ruby Ct SL SL1 ....25 G4
Ruddlesway WDSR SL4 ....34 D5
Rudsworth Cl DTCH/LGLY SL3 ....39 F5
Ruggles-Brise Rd ASHF TW15 ....49 H5
Runnemede Rd EGH TW20 ....47 F5
Runnymede Ct EGH TW20 ....47 G5
Ruscombe Gdns
  DTCH/LGLY SL3 ....37 E4
Rusham Park Av EGH TW20 ....51 F2
Rusham Rd EGH TW20 ....51 F2
The Rushes MDHD SL6 ....3 K7
Rushington Av MDHD SL6 ....22 B3
Rushmere Pl EGH TW20 ....51 E1
Ruskin Rd STA TW18 ....52 D2
Russell Cl WDSR SL4 ....7 F5
Russell St WDSR SL4 ....7 F5
Russet Cl STWL/WRAY TW19 ....45 H5
Russet Rd MDHD SL6 ....21 G5
Rutherford Cl WDSR SL4 ....35 F5
Rutland Av SL SL1 ....16 A5
Rutland Ga MDHD SL6 ....21 G2
Rutland Pl MDHD SL6 ....21 G2
Rutland Rd MDHD SL6 ....2 A6
Rycroft WDSR SL4 ....41 F2
Rydal Wy EGH TW20 ....51 H3
The Ryde STA TW18 ....53 F4
Rydings STA TW18 ....41 F2
Rye Cl MDHD SL6 ....21 H5
Rye Ct SL SL1 * ....5 G6
Ryhstone Cl MDHD SL6 ....21 G5
Ryvers End DTCH/LGLY SL3 ....28 B5
Ryvers Rd DTCH/LGLY SL3 ....28 B5

## S

Sadlers Ms MDHD SL6 ....3 J4
Saffron Cl DTCH/LGLY SL3 ....37 F5
St Adrian's Cl MDHD SL6 ....7 H4
St Albans Cl WDSR SL4 ....7 H4
St Alban's Rd WDSR SL4 ....7 H4
St Andrews Av WDSR SL4 ....41 F1
St Andrew's Cl
  STWL/WRAY TW19 ....44 A4
St Andrew's Crs WDSR SL4 ....43 E5
St Andrew's Wy SL SL1 ....24 D2
St Anne's Av
  STWL/WRAY TW19 ....49 H1
St Bernards Rd DTCH/LGLY SL3 ....27 G5
St Chad's Rd MDHD SL6 ....21 E1
Saint-Cloud Wy MDHD SL6 ....3 F4
St Columba's Cl MDHD SL6 ....21 F4
St Cuthbert's Cl EGH ....50 D2
St David's Cl IVER SLO ....19 F1
St David's Dr EGH TW20 ....50 C5
St Elmo Cl SLN SL2 ....16 B4
St Elmo Crs SLN SL2 ....16 B4
St George's Cl WDSR SL4 ....35 E5
St George's Crs SL SL1 ....24 D2
St Ives Rd MDHD SL6 ....3 G5
St James Pl SL SL1 * ....5 G4
St James Wk IVER SLO ....29 G4
St Johns Ct EGH TW20 ....51 G1
St Johns Dr WDSR SL4 ....41 F1
St Johns Rd SLN SL2 ....5 H2
  WDSR SL4 ....41 E1
St Jude's Cl EGH TW20 ....50 C1
St Jude's Rd EGH TW20 ....46 C5
St Laurence Wy SL SL1 ....5 C6
St Leonard's Av WDSR SL4 ....40 D3
St Leonard's HI WDSR SL4 ....40 D3
St Leonard's Rd WDSR SL4 ....7 F7
  WDSR SL4 ....43 E5
St Leonards Wk IVER SLO ....29 H5
St Luke's Rd MDHD SL6 ....2 E4
  WDSR SL4 ....43 E5

St Margaret's Cl IVER SLO ....19 F2
St Margaret's Rd MDHD SL6 ....21 F1
St Mark's Cl WDSR SL4 ....7 H3
St Mark's Crs MDHD SL6 ....21 F1
St Mark's Pl WDSR SL4 ....7 H3
St Mark's Rd MDHD SL6 ....2 E5
  EGH ....6 E6
St Martin's Ct ASHF TW15 ....53 G1
St Mary's Av S
  TWL/WRAY TW19 ....49 H1
St Mary's Cl MDHD SL6 ....28 A1
St Mary's Crs
  STWL/WRAY TW19 ....49 H1
St Mary's Rd DTCH/LGLY SL3 ....28 A4
St Marys Wk MDHD SL6 ....3 F3
St Michael's Ct SLN SL2 ....14 D4
St Nazaire Cl EGH TW20 ....52 A1
St Olave's Ct STA TW18 ....52 D3
St Patrick's Cl MDHD SL6 ....21 E4
St Pauls Av SL SL1 ....23 H4
St Paul's Rd STA TW18 ....52 B1
St Peter's Cl SL SL1 ....14 B4
  STA TW18 ....52 D2
St Peter's Rd MDHD SL6 ....11 H3
St Pinnock Av STA TW18 ....53 E4
St Thomas Wk DTCH/LGLY SL3 ....28 A3
Salisbury Av MDHD SL6 ....16 A4
Salters Cl MDHD SL6 ....3 H4
Salters' Rd MDHD SL6 ....3 H4
Salt Hill Av SL SL1 ....26 A3
Salt Hill Dr SL SL1 ....4 A3
Salt Hill Wy SL SL1 ....26 A3
Sampsons Gn SLN SL2 ....15 F3
Sandisplatt Rd MDHD SL6 ....21 E2
Sanders End SLN SL2 ....15 H4
Sandown Rd SL SL1 ....15 F5
Sandringham Ct SL SL1 ....24 D1
Sandringham Dr ASHF TW15 ....49 H5
Sandringham Rd MDHD SL6 ....12 A3
Sands Farm Dr SL SL1 ....14 C4
Sandy Md MDHD SL6 ....33 E2
Sarsby Dr STWL/WRAY TW19 ....47 G5
Savill Ms EGH TW20 ....50 D2
Savoy Ct MDHD SL6 ....12 B4
Sawyers Cl MDHD SL6 ....31 E1
  WDSR SL4 ....35 E4
Sawyers Crs MDHD SL6 ....30 D1
Saxon Cl DTCH/LGLY SL3 ....28 B4
Saxon Gdns MDHD SL6 ....15 F3
Saxon Wy WDSR SL4 ....32 A5
Scafell Rd SLN SL2 ....15 F5
Scarborough Wy SL SL1 ....25 H4
Scholars Wk DTCH/LGLY SL3 ....28 D2
School La EGH TW20 ....51 G1
  MDHD SL6 ....8 B3
  MDHD SL6 ....9 H3
  MDHD SL6 ....12 A4
  SLN SL2 ....26 D2
Schroder Ct EGH TW20 ....50 B1
Scots Cl STWL/WRAY TW19 ....49 H2
Seacourt Rd DTCH/LGLY SL3 ....38 D1
Second Crs SL SL1 ....16 A5
Sefton Cl SL SL1 ....16 D1
Selwyn Cl WDSR SL4 ....40 D1
Severn Crs DTCH/LGLY SL3 ....38 D2
Seymour Cl MDHD SL6 ....20 D5
Seymour Rd SL SL1 ....4 A4
Shackleton Rd SL SL1 ....4 E1
Shaftesbury Crs STA TW18 ....53 H4
Shaggy Calf La SLN SL2 ....27 E2
Sharney Av DTCH/LGLY SL3 ....28 D5
The Shaw MDHD SL6 ....20 C3
Sheehy Wy SLN SL2 ....27 F2
Sheepcote Rd WDSR SL4 ....35 G2
  WDSR SL4 ....41 E1
Sheephouse Rd MDHD SL6 ....12 D3
Sheet St WDSR SL4 ....7 H5
Sheet Street Rd WDSR SL4 ....43 G4
Sheffield Rd SL SL1 ....26 A1
Shelley Cl DTCH/LGLY SL3 ....38 C2
Shenstone Dr SL SL1 ....24 D1
Sherborne Cl DTCH/LGLY SL3 ....39 G5
Sherbourne Dr MDHD SL6 ....21 G5
Shergold Wy MDHD SL6 ....9 F4
Sherman Rd SL SL1 ....16 C5
Sherwood Cl DTCH/LGLY SL3 ....28 A5
Sherwood Dr MDHD SL6 ....21 G2
Shifford Crs MDHD SL6 ....12 A3
Shirley Av WDSR SL4 ....35 F5
Shirley Rd MDHD SL6 ....21 G3
Shoppenhangers Rd
  MDHD ....21 F5
Shop Rd WDSR SL4 * ....34 C4
Shoreham Ri SLN SL2 ....14 D4
Shortfern SLN SL2 ....16 D5
Shortwood Av STA TW18 ....49 F4
Shottesbrooke Pk MDHD SL6 ....30 B5
The Sidings STA TW18 ....49 H5
Sidney Rd STA TW18 ....49 E5
  WDSR SL4 ....40 C2
Silco Dr MDHD SL6 ....21 E5
Silver Cl MDHD SL6 ....21 E3
Silverdale Ct STA TW18 * ....53 F1
Silvertrees Dr MDHD SL6 ....21 E1
Simmons Cl DTCH/LGLY SL3 ....38 C1
Simmons Pl STA TW18 ....52 C1
Simons Wk EGH TW20 ....50 C3
Simpson Cl MDHD SL6 ....3 J5
Skyes Dr STA TW18 ....53 F1
Slough Rd DTCH/LGLY SL3 ....37 E2
  IVER SLO ....19 F3
  SL SL1 ....36 C1
Smewins Rd MDHD SL6 ....30 B5
Smithfield Cl MDHD SL6 ....21 E5
Smithfield Rd MDHD SL6 ....21 E5
Smiths La WDSR SL4 ....41 E1
Snape Sp SL SL1 ....26 C1
Snowball HI MDHD SL6 ....31 F2
Snowcroft DTCH/LGLY SL3 * ....17 G2
Snowden Cl WDSR SL4 ....40 D3
Somerford Cl MDHD SL6 ....3 K5
Somersby Crs MDHD SL6 ....21 H5
Somerset Wy IVER SLO ....29 H4
Somerville Rd WDSR SL4 ....36 A2

Sospel Ct SLN SL2 ....16 A2
South Av EGH TW20 ....52 A2
South Cl SL SL1 ....30 B1
Southcroft EGH TW20 ....50 B1
  SL SL1 ....15 H4
South Field WDSR SL4 ....24 C5
Southfield Gdns SL SL1 ....14 B5
South Gn SL SL1 ....4 D1
Southlea Rd WDSR SL4 ....43 G2
South Meadow La WDSR SL4 ....6 E1
South Rd EGH TW20 ....2 D6
  SL SL1 ....52 D1
South Vw WDSR SL4 ....36 A2
Southwood Sp DTCH/LGLY SL3 ....29 E4
Southwood Gdns MDHD SL6 ....9 E5
Southwood Rd MDHD SL6 ....9 E5
Spackmans Wy SL SL1 ....26 A5
Spencer Gdns EGH TW20 ....50 D1
Spencer Rd MDHD SL6 ....28 B5
Spencers Cl MDHD SL6 ....11 G5
Spencers La MDHD SL6 ....11 G5
Spencers Rd MDHD SL6 ....11 G5
The Spens MDHD SL6 ....3 F3
Sperling Rd MDHD SL6 ....12 B4
Spinners Wk WDSR SL4 ....7 F5
Spinney SLN SL2 ....16 C5
Spitfire Cl DTCH/LGLY SL3 * ....38 C2
Springate Rd DTCH/LGLY SL3 ....28 A4
Spring Av EGH TW20 ....51 E2
Spring Cl MDHD SL6 ....12 B3
Springfield Cl WDSR SL4 ....6 D7
Springfield Pk MDHD SL6 ....32 D2
Springfield Rd DTCH/LGLY SL3 ....28 A4
  WDSR SL4 ....6 D7
Spring HI MDHD SL6 ....22 A5
Spring La MDHD SL6 ....8 B4
  SL SL1 ....25 F3
Spring Ri EGH TW20 ....51 E2
The Spur SL SL1 ....25 H4
Stafferton Wy MDHD SL6 ....3 G7
Stafford Av SLN SL2 ....16 A4
Stafford Cl MDHD SL6 ....24 B1
Stainash Crs STA TW18 ....53 F1
Stainash Pde STA TW18 * ....53 F1
Staines By-Pass
  STWL/WRAY TW19 ....48 C5
Staines Rd STA TW18 ....52 D5
  STWL/WRAY TW19 ....47 F2
Stamford Rd MDHD SL6 ....21 G2
Stanhope Rd SL SL1 ....24 D1
Stanley Gn West
  DTCH/LGLY SL3 ....38 B1
Stanton Wy DTCH/LGLY SL3 ....38 D2
Stanwell Moor Rd
  STWL/WRAY TW19 ....49 F5
Stanwell New Rd STA TW18 ....49 G5
Stanwell Rd DTCH/LGLY SL3 ....44 D2
Startins La MDHD SL6 ....8 C2
Starwood Ct DTCH/LGLY SL3 ....27 G5
Station Ap MDHD SL6 ....3 F4
  STA TW18 ....53 E1
Station Crs ASHF TW15 ....49 H5
Station Pde MDHD SL6 * ....9 F5
Station Rd DTCH/LGLY SL3 ....27 G5
  EGH TW20 ....51 G1
  MDHD SL6 ....3 G5
  MDHD SL6 ....9 F5
  SL SL1 ....25 E1
  STWL/WRAY TW19 ....44 B5
Staunton Rd SLN SL2 ....16 B5
Stephen Cl EGH TW20 ....52 A2
Stephenson Ct SL SL1 * ....5 H4
Stephenson Dr WDSR SL4 ....42 D1
Stewart Av SL SL1 ....16 D5
Stewart Cl MDHD SL6 ....22 A2
Stile Rd DTCH/LGLY SL3 ....37 H1
Stirling Cl WDSR SL4 ....40 D1
Stirling Gv MDHD SL6 ....11 G5
Stirling Rd SLN SL2 ....15 F3
Stockdales Rd WDSR SL4 ....35 F1
Stockwells MDHD SL6 ....15 F4
Stoke Court Dr SLN SL2 ....16 C1
Stoke Gdns SL SL1 ....12 A5
Stoke Gn SLN SL2 ....17 E4
Stoke Park Av SLN SL2 ....16 A3
Stoke Poges La SL SL1 ....4 C2
Stoke Rd SL SL1 ....17 E5
Stokesay SL SL1 ....25 H2
Stompits Rd MDHD SL6 ....32 D3
Stomp Rd SL SL1 ....26 D5
Stonebridge Fld WDSR SL4 ....35 H2
Stonecroft Av IVER SLO ....20 B3
Stonefield Pk MDHD SL6 ....21 G1
Stone House La MDHD SL6 ....8 C1
Stoneyland Ct EGH TW20 ....52 A1
Stoneylands Rd EGH TW20 ....51 F1
Stoney La SL SL1 ....14 A5
Stoney Meade SL SL1 ....25 H3
Stornaway Rd DTCH/LGLY SL3 ....39 E1
Stour Cl SL SL1 ....25 H5
Stovell Rd WDSR SL4 ....35 E3
Stowe Rd SL SL1 ....25 G2
Straight Rd WDSR SL4 ....43 F5
Strande La MDHD SL6 ....9 F5
Strande View Wk MDHD SL6 ....9 F5
Stranraer Gdns SL SL1 ....4 D3
Stratfield Rd SL SL1 ....25 H2
Stratford Cl SLN SL2 ....14 D4
Stratford Gdns MDHD SL6 ....21 G4
Streamside SL SL1 ....15 H5
Strodes College La EGH TW20 ....51 F1
Strode St EGH TW20 ....47 G5
Stroma Ct SL SL1 ....24 D2
Stroud Cl WDSR SL4 ....40 D3
Stroud Farm Rd MDHD SL6 ....30 C5
Stuart Cl WDSR SL4 ....41 F1
Stuart Wy STA TW18 ....53 F2
  WDSR SL4 ....41 F1
Stubbles La MDHD SL6 ....8 A4
Sturt Gn MDHD SL6 ....32 A3
Suffolk Cl SL SL1 ....24 D1

Suffolk Rd MDHD SL6 ....21 H4
Sumburgh Wy SL SL1 ....16 B5
Summerfield SL SL1 ....25 H5
Summerleaze Rd MDHD SL6 ....12 C4
Summers Rd SL SL1 ....14 C3
Sunbury Rd WDSR SL4 ....7 G1
Sun Cl WDSR SL4 ....7 G1
Sunderland Rd MDHD SL6 ....11 F5
Sun La MDHD SL6 ....2 E4
Surly Hall Wk WDSR SL4 ....35 F5
Surrey Av SL SL1 ....16 A5
Sussex Cl SL SL1 ....5 J6
Sussex Keep SL SL1 * ....5 J5
Sussex Pl SL SL1 ....5 J5
Sutton Av DTCH/LGLY SL3 ....27 G4
Sutton Cl MDHD SL6 ....9 H4
  MDHD SL6 ....21 G5
Sutton La DTCH/LGLY SL3 ....38 D3
Sutton Pl DTCH/LGLY SL3 ....38 D3
Sutton Rd MDHD SL6 ....9 H4
Swabey Rd DTCH/LGLY SL3 ....38 D3
Swallow Cl STA TW18 ....48 D5
Swallow La MDHD SL6 ....19 F3
Swallowdale IVER SLO ....19 F3
Swallowfield EGH TW20 ....50 B2
Swallow St IVER SLO ....19 F3
Swan Rd IVER SLO ....19 H5
Sweeps Ditch Cl STA TW18 ....53 E2
Sweeps La EGH TW20 ....51 F1
Switchback Cl MDHD SL6 ....11 H3
Switchback Rd North
  MDHD SL6 ....12 A2
Switchback Rd South
  MDHD SL6 ....11 H3
The Switchback MDHD SL6 ....11 H3
Sycamore Wk DTCH/LGLY SL3 ....28 A1
  EGH TW20 ....50 B2
Sydney Gv SL SL1 ....26 A1
Syke Cluan IVER SLO ....29 G4
Syke Ings IVER SLO ....29 G5
Sykes Rd SL SL1 ....25 H1
Sylvester Rd MDHD SL6 ....12 A3

## T

Talbot Av DTCH/LGLY SL3 ....28 B5
Talbot Pl DTCH/LGLY SL3 ....37 G5
Talbot Rd ASHF TW15 ....53 H1
Talbots Dr MDHD SL6 ....12 B1
Tall Trees DTCH/LGLY SL3 ....39 G5
Tamarisk Wy SL SL1 ....25 H4
Tamar Wy DTCH/LGLY SL3 ....38 D2
Tangier La WDSR SL4 ....7 G1
Taplow Rd MDHD SL6 ....2 A1
Tarbay La WDSR SL4 ....40 B1
Tatchbrook Cl MDHD SL6 ....12 A3
Tavistock Cl MDHD SL6 ....21 E1
  STA TW18 ....53 H3
Taylors Ct MDHD SL6 ....11 F5
Teesdale Rd SLN SL2 ....15 F5
Telford Dr SL SL1 ....25 G4
Tempest Rd EGH TW20 ....52 A2
Templedene Av STA TW18 ....53 F3
Temple Gdns STA TW18 ....52 D4
Temple Rd WDSR SL4 ....7 F6
Ten Acre La EGH TW20 ....52 A5
Tennyson Wy SL SL1 ....15 E4
Terry's La MDHD SL6 ....1 F5
Testwood Rd WDSR SL4 ....34 D5
Thames Av WDSR SL4 ....7 G3
Thames Crs MDHD SL6 ....12 D4
Thamesgate STA TW18 ....53 F5
Thames Md WDSR SL4 ....35 E5
Thames Pth EGH TW20 ....47 E3
  MDHD SL6 ....3 H4
  STA TW18 ....48 C4
Thames Rd DTCH/LGLY SL3 ....38 D1
  WDSR SL4 ....34 C4
Thames St STA TW18 ....52 D1
  WDSR SL4 ....7 H3
Thatchers Dr MDHD SL6 ....21 E3
Thicket Gv MDHD SL6 ....20 D1
Thickthorne La STA TW18 ....53 G3
Third Crs SL SL1 ....16 A5
Thirkleby Cl SL SL1 ....26 A3
Thirlmere Av SL SL1 ....14 D5
Thirlmere Ct EGH TW20 ....51 H3
Thompson Cl DTCH/LGLY SL3 ....38 C1
Thornbridge Rd IVER SLO ....19 E1
Thorncroft EGH TW20 ....50 C3
Thorndike SLN SL2 ....15 G5
Thorn Dr DTCH/LGLY SL3 ....28 A3
Thorney La North IVER SLO ....29 H1
Thorney La South IVER SLO ....29 H4
Thorpe Lea Rd EGH TW20 ....51 H5
Thorpe Rd STA TW18 ....52 B2
Thorpe Cl STA TW18 ....52 C5
Three Castles Pth WDSR SL4 ....7 J7
  WDSR SL4 ....43 F3
Thrift La MDHD SL6 ....31 H2
Thurlby Wy MDHD SL6 ....21 H5
Thurston Rd SL SL1 ....26 B1
Tilbury Wk DTCH/LGLY SL3 ....28 D5
Tilstone Av WDSR SL4 ....40 D1
Tilstone Cl WDSR SL4 ....35 E1
Timbers Wk MDHD SL6 ....21 F3
Timsway STA TW18 ....52 D1
Tinkers La WDSR SL4 ....40 D1
Tinsey Cl EGH TW20 ....51 H1
Tintern Ct SL SL1 ....25 H1
Tite HI EGH TW20 ....50 D1
Tithe Barn Dr MDHD SL6 ....33 G2
Tithe Cl MDHD SL6 ....33 E2
Tithe La STWL/WRAY TW19 ....44 B5
Tockley Rd SL SL1 ....14 B2
Tollgate MDHD SL6 ....12 E2
Tomlin Rd SL SL1 ....15 E4
Topaz Cl SL SL1 ....25 H5
Torin Ct EGH TW20 ....50 C1
Torquay Sp SL SL1 ....15 H5
Torridge Rd DTCH/LGLY SL3 ....38 D3

## Index - featured places

## Acknowledgements

Post Office is a registered trademark of Post Office Ltd. in the UK and other countries.

ols address data provided by Education Direct.

station information supplied by Johnsons

way street data provided by © Tele Atlas N.V. Tele Atlas

en centre information provided by

en Centre Association     Britains best garden centres

ale Garden Centres

tatement on the front cover of this atlas is sourced, selected and quoted
a reader comment and feedback form received in 2004.

**Notes**

# **AA** | **Street by Street** QUESTIONNAIRE

**Dear Atlas User**
**Your comments, opinions and recommendations are very important to us.**
**So please help us to improve our street atlases by taking a few minutes**
**to complete this simple questionnaire.**

You do not need a stamp (unless posted outside the UK). If you do not want to remove
this page from your street atlas, then photocopy it or write your answers on a plain sheet
of paper.

**Send to: The Editor, AA Street by Street, FREEPOST SCE 4598,**
**Basingstoke RG21 4GY**

## ABOUT THE ATLAS...

**Which city/town/county did you buy?**

_____

**Are there any features of the atlas or mapping that you find particularly useful?**

_____
_____
_____

**Is there anything we could have done better?**

_____
_____
_____

**Why did you choose an AA Street by Street atlas?**

_____
_____
_____

**Did it meet your expectations?**

**Exceeded** ☐   **Met all** ☐   **Met most** ☐   **Fell below** ☐

Please give your reasons

_____
_____
_____
_____
_____

**Where did you buy it?**

**For what purpose?** (please tick all applicable)

To use in your own local area ☐   To use on business or at work ☐

Visiting a strange place ☐   In the car ☐   On foot ☐

**Other** (please state)

## LOCAL KNOWLEDGE...

**Local knowledge is invaluable. Whilst every attempt has been made to make the information contained in this atlas as accurate as possible, should you notice any inaccuracies, please detail them below (if necessary, use a blank piece of paper) or e-mail us at *streetbystreet@theAA.com***

## ABOUT YOU...

**Name (Mr/Mrs/Ms)**

**Address**

**Postcode**

**Daytime tel no**                **Mobile tel no**

**E-mail address**

Please only give us your e-mail address and mobile phone number if you wish to hear from us about other products and services from the AA and partners by e-mail or text or mms.

**Which age group are you in?**

**Under 25** ☐   **25-34** ☐   **35-44** ☐   **45-54** ☐   **55-64** ☐   **65+** ☐

**Are you an AA member?   YES** ☐   **NO** ☐

**Do you have Internet access?   YES** ☐   **NO** ☐

The information we hold about you will be used to provide the product(s) and service(s) requested and for identification, account administration, analysis, and fraud/loss prevention purposes. More details about how that information is used is in our Privacy Statement, which you will find under the heading "Personal information" in our Terms and Conditions and on our website. Copies are available from us by post, by contacting our Data Protection Manager at AA, Fanum House, Basing View, Hampshire, Basingstoke RG21 4EA.

We may want to contact you about other products and services provided by us or our partners but please tick the box if you DO NOT wish to hear about such products and services from us by mail or telephone. ☐

Thank you for taking the time to complete this questionnaire. Please send it to us as soon as possible, and remember, you do not need a stamp (unless posted outside the UK).                ML180x